Django for Beginners

GW00645497

Build websites with Python & Django

William S. Vincent

Django for Beginners

Build websites with Python & Django

William S. Vincent

learndjango.com

ISBN-13: 978-1735467207

Also By William S. Vincent

Django for APIs

Django for Professionals

Contents

Introduction

Welcome to *Django for Beginners*, a project-based approach to learning web development with the Django[1] web framework. In this book you will build five progressively more complex web applications, starting with a simple *Hello, World* app, progressing to a *Pages* app, a *Message Board* app, a *Blog* app with forms and user accounts, and finally a *Newspaper* app that uses a custom user model, email integration, foreign keys, authorization, permissions, and more. By the end of this book you should feel confident creating your own Django projects from scratch using current best practices.

Django is a free, open source web framework written in the Python programming language. First released in 2005, Django has been in continuous development since then and today powers many of the largest websites in the world including Instagram, Pinterest, Bitbucket, and Disqus. At the same time, it is flexible enough to be a popular choice for early-stage startups and side projects.

Why Django

A "web framework" is a collection of tools that abstract away much of the difficulty—and repetition—inherent in web development. For example, most websites need the same basic functionality: the ability to connect to a database, set URL routes, display content on a page, handle security properly, and so on. Rather than recreate all of this from scratch, programmers over the years have created web frameworks in all the major programming languages: *Django* in Python, *Rails* in Ruby, and *Laravel* in PHP among many, many others.

Django inherited Python's "batteries-included" approach and includes out-of-the box support for common tasks in web development, including:

- user authentication
- testing

---
[1]https://djangoprojcct.com

- database models, forms, URL routes, and templates
- admin interface
- security and performance upgrades
- support for multiple database backends

This approach allows web developers to focus on what makes a web application unique rather than reinventing the wheel every time.

In contrast, some web frameworks like Flask[2] adopt a *microframework* approach of providing only the bare minimum required for a simple web page. Flask is far more lightweight than Django and allows for maximum flexibility, however this comes at a cost to the developer. To build even a basic website requires adding a dozen or more third-party packages, which may or may not be up-to-date. And the resulting Flask project structure often varies widely, making it more difficult to move between projects and maintain best practices within the community.

Django remains under active development[3] with a regular release schedule of monthly security/bug fixes and a major new release every 8 months. Millions of programmers have already used Django to build their websites. It doesn't make sense to repeat the same code–and mistakes–when a large community of brilliant developers has already solved these problems for us.

The Django community is also constantly adding new features and security improvements. And best of all, it's written in the wonderfully readable yet still powerful Python programming language. In short, if you're building a website from scratch Django is a fantastic choice.

Why This Book

I wrote this book because while Django is extremely well documented there is a severe lack of beginner-friendly tutorials available. When I first learned Django years ago, I struggled to even complete the official polls tutorial[4]. Why was this so hard I remember thinking?

With more experience, I now recognize that the writers of the Django docs faced a difficult choice: they could emphasize Django's ease-of-use or its depth, but not both. They choose the

---

[2]https://flask.palletsprojects.com/en/2.0.x/
[3]https://www.djangoproject.com/download/#supported-versions
[4]https://docs.djangoproject.com/en/4.0/intro/tutorial01/

latter and as a professional developer I appreciate the choice, but as a beginner I found it so... frustrating! My goal with this book is to fill in the gaps and showcase how beginner-friendly Django really can be.

Prerequisites

Django for Beginners is written for Django 4.0 and Python 3.10. All the code examples work with these versions. By the time you read this, there may be newer versions of both Django and Python available. In general, you should always strive to be on the latest version of Django and Python. As both are mature technologies, any issues that arise in the future as a result will be relatively minor.

You don't need previous Python or web development experience to complete this book. It is intentionally written so that even a total beginner can follow along and feel the magic of writing their own web applications from scratch. However, if you are serious about a career in web development, you will eventually need to invest the time to properly learn Python, HTML, and CSS. A list of recommended resources for further study is included in the Conclusion.

Book Structure

The book begins by demonstrating how to configure a local development environment for both Windows and macOS in **Chapter 1**. The command line is covered in depth along with Git, text editors, and proper installation of Python and Django.

In **Chapter 2** we build our first project, a minimal *Hello, World* app that demonstrates how to set up new Django projects. Because establishing good software practices is important, we'll also save our work with Git and upload a copy to a remote code repository on GitHub.

In **Chapter 3** we make, test, and deploy a *Pages* app that introduces templates and class-based views. Templates are how Django allows for DRY (Don't Repeat Yourself) development with HTML and CSS while class-based views are quite powerful yet require a minimal amount of code. We also add our first tests and deploy to Heroku's free tier. Using platform-as-a-service providers like Heroku transforms deployment from a painful, time-consuming process into something that takes just a few mouse clicks.

In **Chapter 4** we build our first database-backed project which is a *Message Board* app. Django provides a powerful ORM (Object-Relational-Mapper) that translates our Python code into the necessary SQL for multiple different backends. We'll explore the built-in admin app which provides a graphical way to interact with our data and can be even used as a CMS (Content Management System) similar to Wordpress. Of course, we also write tests for all our code, store a remote copy on GitHub, and deploy to Heroku.

In **Chapters 5-7** we're ready for a *Blog* app that implements CRUD (Create-Read-Update-Delete) functionality. By using Django's generic class-based views we only have to write only a small amount of actual code for this. Then we'll add forms and integrate Django's built-in user authentication system for sign up, log in, and log out functionality.

The remainder of the book, **Chapters 8-16**, is dedicated to building a robust *Newspaper* site, starting with the introduction to custom user models in **Chapter 8**, a Django best practice that is rarely addressed in tutorials. **Chapter 9** covers user authentication, **Chapter 10** adds Bootstrap for styling, and **Chapters 11-12** implement password reset and change via email. With **Chapters 13-15** we add articles and comments along with proper permissions and authorizations. We even learn some tricks for customizing the admin to display our growing data.

Chapter 16 covers production-ready deployment through the use of environment variables and several additional packages. And the **Conclusion** provides an overview of the major concepts introduced in the book and a list of recommended resources for further learning.

The book's structure is very deliberate: each chapter introduces a new concept and reinforces past teachings. I highly recommend reading the book in order, even if you're eager to skip ahead. Later chapters won't cover previous material in the same depth as earlier chapters.

By the end of this book you'll have a solid understanding of how Django works, the ability to build apps on your own, and the background needed to fully take advantage of additional resources for learning intermediate and advanced Django techniques.

Book Layout

There are many code examples in this book, which are denoted as follows:

Code

```
# This is Python code
print("Hello, World!")
```

For brevity we will use three dots, ..., to denote existing code that remains unchanged in a longer code example. For example, in the function below, the previous content is unchanged and the `print()` statement has been added. In these cases there will also be a comment, `# new`, indicating where the new code has been added.

Code

```
def make_my_website:
    ...
    print("All done!")   # new
```

Advice on Getting Stuck

Getting stuck on an issue is part of being a programmer. It happens to everyone at every level. The only thing that changes is the difficulty of the question being tackled. Part of learning how to be a better developer is accepting this frustration and learning how to find help, ask targeted questions, and determine when you need to take a walk around the block to clear your head versus being truly stuck on something.

The good news is that whatever error you are having, it is likely that you are not the first! Copy and pasting your error into a search engine like Google or DuckDuckGo will typically bring up something from StackOverflow or a personal blog detailing the exact same issue. In fact, experienced programmers often joke that the only thing that separates them from junior programmers is their ability to Google more quickly towards an answer. There is some truth to this.

Not everything you read online can be trusted, of course, and with experience you will develop the context to see how the pieces of Django and code in general fit together.

What to do if you are stuck on something in this book? As a first step, I recommend carefully checking your code against what is in the book. If still stuck, you can look at the official source code which is available on GitHub[5]. A common error is subtle white spacing differences that are almost impossible to detect to the naked eye. You can try copy and pasting the official source code if you suspect this might be the issue.

The next step is to walk away from the computer for a bit or even sleep on the problem. It's amazing what a small amount of rest and distance will do to your mind when it comes to solving problems.

There are two fantastic online resources where the Django community gathers to ask and answer questions. The first is the official Django Forum[6] and the second is the Django Users Google Group[7]. Both are a good next step if you need additional help.

Community

The success of Django owes as much to its community as it does the technological achievement of the framework itself. "Come for the framework, stay for the community" is a common saying among Django developers. It extends to the technical development of Django, which happens online via the django-developers[8], the non-profit Django Software Foundation[9] that oversees Django itself, annual DjangoCon conferences, and local meetups where developers gather to share knowledge and insights.

No matter what your level of technical expertise becoming involved in Django itself is a great way to learn, to meet other developers, and to enhance your own reputation.

Conclusion

In the next chapter you'll learn how to properly set up your computer and create your first Django project. Let's begin!

---

[5]https://github.com/wsvincent/djangoforbeginners
[6]https://forum.djangoproject.com/
[7]https://groups.google.com/g/django-users
[8]https://docs.djangoproject.com/en/dev/internals/mailing-lists/#django-developers-mailing-list
[9]https://www.djangoproject.com/foundation/

Chapter 1: Initial Set Up

This chapter covers how to properly configure your Windows or macOS computer to work on Django projects. We start with an overview of the *Command Line*, a powerful text-only interface that developers use extensively to install and configure Django projects. Then we install the latest version of Python, learn how to create dedicated virtual environments, and install Django. As a final step, we will explore using Git for version control and working with a text editor. By the end of this chapter you will have created your first Django project from scratch and more importantly be able to create and modify new Django projects in just a few keystrokes.

The Command Line

If you have ever seen a television show or movie where a hacker is furiously typing into a black window: that's the command line. It is an alternative to the mouse or finger-based graphical user interface familiar to most computer users. An everyday computer user will never need to use the command line but software developers do because certain tasks can only be done with it. These include running programs, installing software, using Git for version control, or connecting to servers in the cloud. With a little practice, most developers find that the command line is actually a faster and more powerful way to navigate and control a computer.

Given its minimal user interface–just a blank screen and a blinking cursor–the command line is intimidating to newcomers. There is often no feedback after a command has run and it is possible to wipe the contents of an entire computer with a single command if you're not careful: no warning will pop up! As a result, the command line must be used with caution. Make sure not to blindly copy and paste commands you find online; only rely on trusted resources for any command you do not fully understand.

In practice, multiple terms are used to refer to the command line: Command Line Interface (CLI), console, terminal, shell, or prompt. Technically speaking, the *terminal* is the program that opens up a new window to access the command line, a *console* is a text-based application, the *shell* is the program that runs commands on the underlying operating system, and the *prompt* is where commands are typed and run. It is easy to be confused by these terms initially but they all essentially mean the same thing: the command line is where we run and execute text-only commands on our computer.

On Windows, the built-in terminal and shell are both called *PowerShell*. To access it, locate the taskbar on the bottom of the screen next to the Windows button and type in "powershell" to launch the app. It will open a new window with a dark blue background and a blinking cursor after the > prompt. Here is how it looks on my computer.

Shell

```
PS C:\Users\wsv>
```

Before the prompt is PS which refers to PowerShell, the initial C directory of the Windows operating system, followed by the Users directory and the current user which, on my personal computers, is wsv. Your username will obviously be different. At this point, don't worry about what comes to *the left* of the > prompt: it varies depending on each computer and can be customized at a later date. The shorter prompt of > will be used going forward for Windows.

On macOS, the built-in terminal is called appropriately enough *Terminal*. It can be opened via Spotlight: press the Command and space bar keys at the same time and then type in "terminal." Alternatively, open a new Finder window, navigate to the *Applications* directory, scroll down to open the *Utilities* directory, and double-click the application called Terminal. This opens a new screen with a white background by default and a blinking cursor after the % prompt. Don't worry about what comes to *the left* of the % prompt. It varies by computer and can be customized later on.

Shell

```
Wills-Macbook-Pro:~ wsv%
```

If your macOS prompt is $ instead of % that means you are using Bash as the shell. Starting in 2019, macOS switched from *Bash* to *zsh* as the default shell. While most of the commands in this book will work interchangeably, it is recommended to look up online how to change to zsh via System Preferences if your computer still uses Bash.

Shell Commands

There are many available shell commands but most developers rely on the same handful over and over again and look up more complicated ones as needed.

In most cases, the commands for Windows (PowerShell) and macOS are similar. For example, the command whoami returns the computer name/username on Windows and just the username on macOS. As with all shell commands, type the command itself followed by the return key. Note that the # symbol represents a comment and will not be executed on the command line.

Shell

```
# Windows
> whoami
wsv2021/wsv

# macOS
% whoami
wsv
```

Sometimes, however, the shell commands on Windows and macOS are completely different. A good example is the command for outputting a basic "Hello, World!" message to the console. On Windows the command is Write-Host while on macOS the command is echo.

Shell

```
# Windows
> Write-Host "Hello, World!"
Hello, World!

# macOS
% echo "Hello, World!"
Hello, World!
```

A frequent task on the command line is navigating within the computer filesystem. On Windows and macOS the command pwd (print working directory) outputs the current location within the file system.

Shell

```
# Windows
> pwd

Path
----
C:\Users\wsv

# macOS
% pwd
/Users/wsv
```

You can save your Django code anywhere you like but for convenience we will place our code the desktop directory. The command cd (change directory) followed by the intended location works on both systems.

Shell

```
# Windows
> cd onedrive\desktop
> pwd

Path
----
C:\Users\wsv\onedrive\desktop

# macOS
% cd desktop
% pwd
/Users/wsv/desktop
```

Tip: The tab key will autocomplete a command so if you type cd d and then hit tab it will automatically fill in the rest of the name. If there are more than two directories that start with d, hit the tab key again to cycle through them.

To make a new directory use the command mkdir followed by the name. We will create one called code on the Desktop and then within it a new directory called ch1-setup.

Shell

```
# Windows
> mkdir code
> cd code
> mkdir ch1-setup
> cd ch1-setup

# macOS
% mkdir code
% cd codc
% mkdir ch1-setup
% cd ch1-setup
```

You can check that it has been created by looking on your Desktop or running the command `ls`. The full Windows output is slightly longer but is shortened here for conciseness.

Shell

```
# Windows
> ls
testdir

# macOS
% ls
testdir
```

Tip: The `clear` command will clear the Terminal of past commands and outputs so you have a clean slate. The `tab` command autocompletes the line as we've discussed. And the ↑ and ↓ keys cycle through previous commands to save yourself from typing the same thing over and over again.

To exit you could close the Terminal with your mouse but the hacker way is to use use the shell command `exit` instead. This works by default on Windows but on macOS the Terminal preferences need to be changed. At the top of the screen click on `Terminal`, then `Preferences` from the drop down menu. Click on `Profiles` in the top menu and then `Shell` from the list below. There is a radio button for "When the shell exits:". Select "Close the window."

Shell

```
# Windows
> exit

# macOS
% exit
```

Kinda cool, right? With practice, the command line is a far more efficient way to navigate and operate your computer than using a mouse. For this book you don't need to be a command line expert: I will provide the exact instructions to run each time. But if you are curious, a complete list of shell commands for each operating system can be found over at ss64.com.

Install Python 3 on Windows

On Windows, Microsoft hosts a community release of Python 3 in the Microsoft Store. In the search bar on the bottom of your screen type in "python" and click on the best match result. This will automatically launch Python 3.10 on the Microsoft Store. Click on the blue "Get" button to download it.

To confirm Python was installed correctly, open a new Terminal window with PowerShell and then type python --version.

Shell

```
> python --version
Python 3.10.2
```

The result should be at least Python 3.10. Then type python to open the Python interpreter from the command line shell.

Shell

```
> python
Python 3.10.2 (tags/v3.10.2:a58ebcc, Jan 17 2022, 19:00:18)
[MSC v.1929 64 bit (AMD64)] on win32
Type "help", "copyright", "credits", or "license" for more information.
>>>
```

Install Python 3 on Mac

On Mac, the official installer on the Python website is the best approach. In a new browser window go the Python downloads page[10] and click on the button underneath the text "Download the latest version for Mac OS X." As of this writing, that is Python 3.10. The package will be in your Downloads directory. Double click on it which launches the Python Installer and follow through the prompts.

To confirm the download was successful, open up a new Terminal window and type python3 --version.

Shell

```
% python3 --version
Python 3.10.2
```

The result should be at least 3.10. Then type python3 to open the Python interpreter.

---

[10]https://www.python.org/downloads/

Shell

```
% python3
Python 3.10.2 (v3.10.2:a58ebcc701, Jan 13 2022, 14:50:16)
 [Clang 13.0.0 (clang-1300.0.29.30)] on darwin
Type "help", "copyright", "credits" or "license" for more information.
>>>
```

Python Interactive Mode

From the command line typing either `python` on Windows or `python3` on macOS will bring up the Python Interpreter, also known as Python Interactive mode. The new prompt of >>> indicates that you are now inside Python itself and **not** the command line. If you try any of the previous shell commands we ran—`cd`, `ls`, `mkdir`—they will each raise errors. What *will* work is actual Python code. For example, try out both `1 + 1` and `print("Hello Python!")` making sure to hit the `Enter` or `Return` key after each to run them.

Shell

```
>>> 1 + 1
2
>>> print("Hello Python!")
Hello Python!
```

Python's interactive mode is a great way to save time if you want to try out a short bit of Python code. But it has a number of limitations: you can't save your work in a file and writing longer code snippets is cumbersome. As a result, we will spend most of our time writing Python and Django in files using a text editor.

To exit Python from the command line you can type either `exit()` and the `Enter` key or use `Ctrl + z` on Windows or `Ctrl + d` on macOS.

Virtual Environments

Installing the latest version of Python and Django is the correct approach for any new project. But in the real world, it is common that existing projects rely on older versions of each. Consider the following situation: *Project* A uses Django 2.2 but *Project* B uses Django 4.0? By default, Python and Django are installed *globally* on a computer meaning it is quite a pain to install and reinstall different versions every time you want to switch between projects.

Fortunately, there is a straightforward solution. *Virtual environments* allow you to create and manage separate environments for each Python project on the same computer. There are many areas of software development that are hotly debated, but using virtual environments for Python development is not one. **You should use a dedicated virtual environment for each new Python project**.

There are several ways to implement virtual environments but the simplest is with the venv[11] module already installed as part of the Python 3 standard library. To try it out, navigate to the existing ch1-setup directory on your Desktop.

Shell

```
# Windows
> cd onedrive\desktop\code\ch1-setup

# macOS
% cd ~/desktop/code/ch1-setup
```

To create a virtual environment within this new directory use the format python -m venv <name_-of_env> on Windows or python3 -m venv <name_of_env> on macOS. It is up to the developer to choose a proper environment name but a common choice is to call it .venv.

---

[11]https://docs.python.org/3/library/venv.html

Shell

```
# Windows
> python -m venv .venv
> Set-ExecutionPolicy -ExecutionPolicy RemoteSigned -Scope CurrentUser

# macOS
% python3 -m venv .venv
```

If you use the command `ls` to look at our current directory it will appear empty. However the
`.venv` directory *is* there, it's just that it is "hidden" due to the period `.` that precedes the name.
Hidden files and directories are a way for developers to indicate that the contents are important
and should be treated differently than regular files. To view it, try `ls -la` which shows all
directories and files, even hidden ones.

Shell

```
> ls -la
total 0
drwxr-xr-x  3 wsv  staff   96 Dec  12 11:10 .
drwxr-xr-x  3 wsv  staff   96 Dec  12 11:10 ..
drwxr-xr-x  6 wsv  staff  192 Dec  12 11:10 .venv
```

You will see that `.venv` is there and can be accessed via `cd` if desired. In the directory itself is a
copy of the Python interpreter and a few management scripts, but you will not need to use it
directly in this book.

Once created, a virtual environment must be *activated*. On Windows an *Execution Policy* must
be set to enable running scripts. This is a safety precaution. The Python docs[12] recommend
allowing scripts for the `CurrentUser` only, which is what we will do. On macOS there are no
similar restrictions on scripts so it is possible to directly run `source .venv/bin/activate`.

Here is what the full commands look like to create and activate a new virtual environment called
`.venv`:

---

[12]https://docs.python.org/3/library/venv.html

Shell

```
# Windows
> python -m venv .venv
> Set-ExecutionPolicy -ExecutionPolicy RemoteSigned -Scope CurrentUser
> .venv\Scripts\Activate.ps1
(.venv) >

# macOS
% python3 -m venv .venv
% source .venv/bin/activate
(.venv) %
```

The shell prompt now has the environment name (.venv) prefixed which indicates that the virtual environment is active. Any Python packages installed or updated within this location will be confined to the active virtual environment.

To deactivate and leave a virtual environment type deactivate.

Shell

```
# Windows
(.venv) > deactivate
>

# macOS
(.venv) % deactivate
%
```

The shell prompt no longer has the virtual environment name prefixed which means the session is now back to normal.

Install Django

Now that Python is installed and we know how to use virtual environments it is time to install Django for the first time. In the ch1-setup directory reactivate the existing virtual environment.

Shell

```
# Windows
> .venv\Scripts\Activate.ps1
(.venv) >

# macOS
% source .venv/bin/activate
(.venv) %
```

Django is hosted on the Python Package Index (PyPI)[13], a central repository for most Python packages. We will use `pip`, the most popular package installer, which comes included with Python 3. To install the latest version of Django use the command `python -m pip install django~=4.0.0`.

The comparison operator `~=` ensures that subsequent security updates for Django, such as 4.0.1, 4.0.2, and so on are automatically installed. Note that while it is possible to use the shorter version of `pip install <package>`, it is a best practice to use the longer but more explicit form of `python -m pip install <package>` to ensure that the correct version of Python is used. This can be an issue if you have multiple versions of Python installed on your computer.

Shell

```
(.venv) > python -m pip install django~=4.0.0
```

You might see a WARNING message about updating `pip` after running these commands. It's always good to be on the latest version of software and to remove the annoying WARNING message each time you use `pip`. You can either copy and paste the recommended command or run `python -m pip install --upgrade pip` to be on the latest version.

Shell

```
(.venv) > python -m pip install --upgrade pip
```

---

[13] https://pypi.org

First Django Project

A Django project can have almost any name but we will use `django_project` in this book. To create a new Django project use the command `django-admin startproject django_project` .

Shell

```
(.venv) > django-admin startproject django_project .
```

It's worth pausing here to explain why you should add a period (.) to the end of the previous command. If you just run `django-admin startproject django_project` then by default Django will create this directory structure:

Layout

```
django_project/
        ├── django_project
        │       ├── __init__.py
        │       ├── asgi.py
        │       ├── settings.py
        │       ├── urls.py
        │       └── wsgi.py
        ├── manage.py
        └── .venv/
```

Do you see the multiple `django_project` directories? First a top-level `django_project` directory is created and then *another* one within it that contains the files we need for our Django project. This feels redundant to me which is why I prefer adding a period to the end which installs Django in the current directory.

Layout

```
├── django_project
│   ├── __init__.py
│   ├── asgi.py
│   ├── settings.py
│   ├── urls.py
│   └── wsgi.py
├── manage.py
└── .venv/
```

As you progress in your journey learning Django, you'll start to bump up more and more into similar situations where there are different opinions within the Django community on the correct best practice. Django is eminently customizable, which is a great strength, however the tradeoff is that this flexibility comes at the cost of seeming complexity. Generally speaking, it's a good idea to research any such issues that arise, make a decision, and then stick with it!

Now let's confirm everything is working by running Django's internal web server via the `runserver` command. This is suitable for local development purposes, but when it comes time to deploy our project's online we will switch to a more robust WSGI server like *Gunicorn*.

Shell

```
# Windows
(.venv) > python manage.py runserver

# macOS
(.venv) % python3 manage.py runserver

Watching for file changes with StatReloader
Performing system checks...

System check identified no issues (0 silenced).

You have 18 unapplied migration(s). Your project may not work properly until
you apply the migrations for app(s): admin, auth, contenttypes, sessions.
Run 'python manage.py migrate' to apply them.

December 12, 2021 - 15:26:23
Django version 4.0.0, using settings 'django_project.settings'
Starting development server at http://127.0.0.1:8000/
Quit the server with CONTROL-BREAK.
```

Don't worry about the text in red about 18 unapplied migrations. We'll get to that shortly. The important part, for now, is to visit http://127.0.0.1:8000/ in your web browser and make sure the following image is visible:

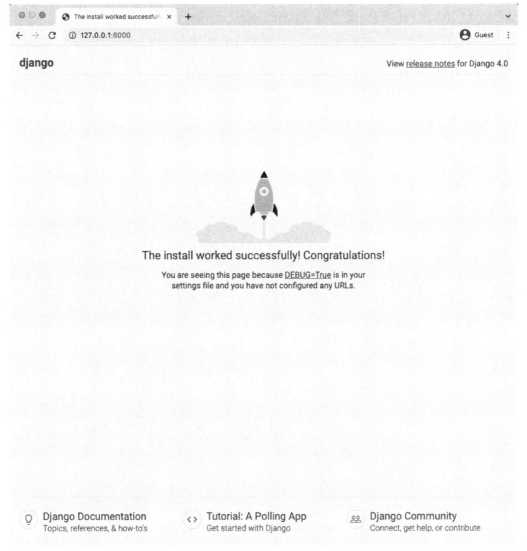

Django welcome page

If you are on Windows you'll see the final line says to use CONTROL-BREAK to quit whereas on macOS it is CONTROL-C. Newer Windows keyboards often do not have a Pause/Break key in which case using the c key usually works.

As a side note, it is also possible to visit `http://localhost:8000` to see the running Django website. There are two ways to visit a local port number on your machine. I default to `127.0.0.1:8000` in this book because that is what Django outputs in the terminal but either is okay to use in practice.

Go ahead and stop the local server with the appropriate command and then exit the virtual environment by typing `deactivate` and hitting `Return`.

Shell

```
# Windows or macOS
(.venv) > deactivate
```

We'll get lots of practice with virtual environments in this book so don't worry if it's a little confusing right now. The basic pattern for any new Django project is to first make and activate a virtual environment, install Django, and then run `startproject`.

It's worth noting that only one virtual environment can be active in a command line tab at a time. In future chapters we will be creating a brand new virtual environment for each new project so either make sure to `deactivate` your current environment or open up a new tab for new projects.

Text Editors

The command line is where we execute commands for our programs but a text editor is where actual code is written. The computer doesn't care what text editor you use–the end result is just code–but a good text editor can provide helpful hints and catch typos for you.

There are many modern text editors available but a very popular one is Visual Studio Code[14], which is free, easy to install, and enjoys widespread popularity. If you're not already using a text editor, download and install VSCode from the official website.

An optional–but highly recommended–additional step is to take advance of the large ecosystem of extensions available on VSCode. On Windows, navigate to `File -> Preferences ->`

---

[14]https://code.visualstudio.com/

Extensions or on macOS `Code -> Preferences -> Extensions`. This launches a search bar for the extensions marketplace. Enter "python" which will bring up the Microsoft extension as the first result. Install it.

A second extension to add is Black[15], which is a Python code formatter that has quickly become the default within the Python community. To install Black, open a Terminal window within VSCode by going to `Terminal -> New Terminal` at the top of the page. In the new terminal window opened at the bottom of the page, type `python -m pip install black`. Next, open up the VSCode settings by navigating to `File -> Preferences -> Settings` on Windows or `Code -> Preferences -> Settings` on macOS. Search for "python formatting provider" and select `black` from the dropdown options. Then search for "format on save" and enable "Editor: Format on Save". Black will now automatically format your code whenever a `*.py` file is saved.

To confirm this is working, use your text editor to create a new file called `hello.py` within the `ch1-setup` directory. located on your Desktop and type in the following using single quotes:

hello.py

```
print('Hello, World!')
```

On save, it should be automatically updated to using double quotes which is Black's default preference[16]: `print("Hello, World!")`. That means everything is working properly.

Install Git

The final step is to install *Git*, a version control system that is indispensable to modern software development. With Git you can collaborate with other developers, track all your work via commits, and revert to any previous version of your code even if you accidentally delete something important!

On Windows, navigate to the official website at `https://git-scm.com/` and click on the "Download" link which should install the proper version for your computer. Save the file and then open your Downloads folder and double click on the file. This will launch the Git for Windows installer.

---

[15]https://pypi.org/project/black/
[16]https://black.readthedocs.io/en/stable/the_black_code_style/current_style.html#strings

Click the "Next" button through most of the early defaults as they are fine and can always be updated later as needed. There are two exceptions however: under "Choosing the default editor used by Git" select VS Code not Vim. And in the section on "Adjusting the name of the initial branch in new repositories" select the option to use "main" as opposed to "master" as the default branch name. Otherwise the recommended defaults are fine and can always be tweaked later if needed.

To confirm Git is installed on Windows, close all current shell windows and then open a new one which will load the changes to our PATH variable. Type in `git --version` which should show it is installed.

Shell

```
# Windows
> git --version
git version 2.33.1.windows.1
```

On macOS, installing Git via Xcode is currently the easiest option. To check if Git is already installed on your computer, type `git --version` in a new terminal window.

Shell

```
# macOS
% git --version
```

If you do not have Git installed, a popup message will ask if you want to install it as part of "command line developer tools." Select "Install" which will load Xcode and its command line tools package. Or if you do not see the message for some reason, type `xcode-select --install` instead to install Xcode directly.

Be aware that Xcode is a very large package so the initial download may take some time. Xcode is primarily designed for building iOS apps but also includes many developer features need on macOS. Once the download is complete close all existing terminal shells, open a new window, and type in `git --version` to confirm the install worked.

Shell

```
# macOS
% git --version
git version 2.30.1 (Apple Git-130)
```

Once Git is installed on your machine we need to do a one-time *system* configuration by declaring the name and email address associated with all your Git commits. We will also set the default branch name to `main`. Within the command line shell type the following two lines. Make sure to update them your name and email address.

Shell

```
> git config --global user.name "Your Name"
> git config --global user.email "yourname@email.com"
> git config --global init.defaultBranch main
```

You can always change these configs later if you desire by retyping the same commands with a new name or email address.

Conclusion

Phew! It is no easy task to configure a software development environment. But fortunately it is a one-time pain and will pay many dividends done the road. We have now learned about the command line, Python interactive mode, installed the latest version of Python, Django and Git, and configured our text editor. Everything is ready for our first Django app in the next chapter.

Chapter 2: Hello World App

In this chapter we will build a Django project that simply says "Hello, World" on the homepage. This is the traditional way to start a new programming language or framework. We'll also work with Git for the first time and deploy our code to GitHub.

If you become stuck at any point, complete source code for this and all future chapters is available online on the official GitHub repo[17] for the book.

Initial Set Up

To begin, open up a new command line shell or use the built-in terminal on VS Code. For the latter click on "Terminal" at the top and then "New Terminal" to bring it up on the bottom of the screen.

Make sure you are not in an existing virtual environment by checking there is nothing in parentheses before your command line prompt. You can even type `deactivate` to be completely sure. Then navigate to the `code` directory on your Desktop and create a `helloworld` directory with the following commands.

---

[17]https://github.com/wsvincent/djangoforbeginners

Shell

```
# Windows
> cd onedrive\desktop\code
> mkdir helloworld
> cd helloworld

# macOS
% cd ~/desktop/code
% mkdir helloworld
% cd helloworld
```

Create a new virtual environment called .venv, activate it, and install Django with Pip as we did in the previous chapter.

Shell

```
# Windows
> python -m venv .venv
> .venv\Scripts\Activate.ps1
(.venv) > python -m pip install django~=4.0.0

# macOS
% python3 -m venv .venv
% source .venv/bin/activate
(.venv) % python3 -m pip install django~=4.0.0
```

Now we'll use the Django startproject command to make a new project called django_project. Don't forget to include the period (.) at the end of the command so that it is installed in our current directory.

Shell

```
(.venv) > django-admin startproject django_project .
```

Let's pause for a moment to examine the default project structure Django has provided for us. You examine this visually if you like by opening the new directory with your mouse on the Desktop. The .venv directory may not be initially visible because it is "hidden" but nonetheless still there.

Code

```
├── django_project
│   ├── __init__.py
│   ├── asgi.py
│   ├── settings.py
│   ├── urls.py
│   └── wsgi.py
├── manage.py
└── .venv/
```

The `.venv` directory was created with our virtual environment but Django has added a `django_-project` directory and a `manage.py` file. Within `django_project` are five new files:

- `__init__.py` indicates that the files in the folder are part of a Python package. Without this file, we cannot import files from another directory which we will be doing a lot of in Django!
- `asgi.py` allows for an optional Asynchronous Server Gateway Interface[18] to be run
- `settings.py` controls our Django project's overall settings
- `urls.py` tells Django which pages to build in response to a browser or URL request
- `wsgi.py` stands for Web Server Gateway Interface[19] which helps Django serve our eventual web pages.

The `manage.py` file is not part of `django_project` but is used to execute various Django commands such as running the local web server or creating a new app.

Let's try out our new project by using Django's lightweight built-in web server for local development purposes. The command we'll use is `runserver` which is located in `manage.py`.

---

[18]https://asgi.readthedocs.io/en/latest/specs/main.html
[19]https://en.wikipedia.org/wiki/Web_Server_Gateway_Interface

Shell

```
# Windows
(.venv) > python manage.py runserver

# macOS
(.venv) % python3 manage.py runserver
```

If you visit http://127.0.0.1:8000/ you should see the following image:

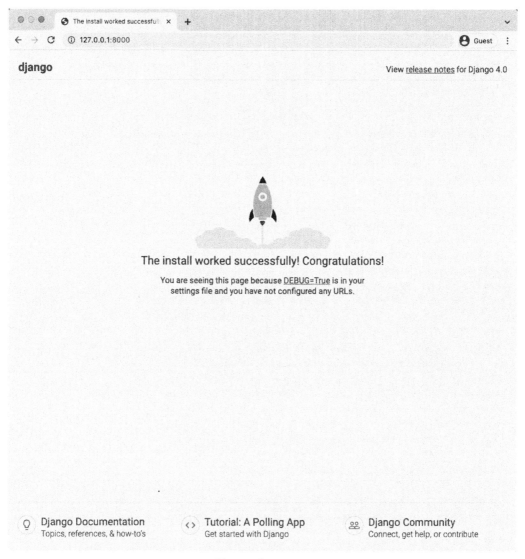

Django welcome page

Note that the full command line output will contain additional information including a warning about 18 `unapplied migrations`. Technically, this warning doesn't matter at this point. Django is complaining that we have not yet "migrated" our initial database. Since we won't actually use a database in this chapter the warning won't affect the end result.

However, since warnings are still annoying to see, we can remove it by first stopping the local server with the command `Control+c` and then running `python manage.py migrate`.

Shell

```
# Windows
> python manage.py migrate

# macOS
% python3 manage.py migrate

Operations to perform:
  Apply all migrations: admin, auth, contenttypes, sessions
Running migrations:
  Applying contenttypes.0001_initial... OK
  Applying auth.0001_initial... OK
  Applying admin.0001_initial... OK
  Applying admin.0002_logentry_remove_auto_add... OK
  Applying admin.0003_logentry_add_action_flag_choices... OK
  Applying contenttypes.0002_remove_content_type_name... OK
  Applying auth.0002_alter_permission_name_max_length... OK
  Applying auth.0003_alter_user_email_max_length... OK
  Applying auth.0004_alter_user_username_opts... OK
  Applying auth.0005_alter_user_last_login_null... OK
  Applying auth.0006_require_contenttypes_0002... OK
  Applying auth.0007_alter_validators_add_error_messages... OK
  Applying auth.0008_alter_user_username_max_length... OK
  Applying auth.0009_alter_user_last_name_max_length... OK
  Applying auth.0010_alter_group_name_max_length... OK
  Applying auth.0011_update_proxy_permissions... OK
  Applying auth.0012_alter_user_first_name_max_length... OK
  Applying sessions.0001_initial... OK
```

What Django has done here is create a SQLite database and migrated its built-in apps provided for us. This is represented by the new file `db.sqlite3` in our directly.

Code

```
├── django_project
│   ├── __init__.py
│   ├── asgi.py
│   ├── settings.py
│   ├── urls.py
│   └── wsgi.py
├── db.sqlite3   # new
├── manage.py
└── .venv/
```

For now, if you execute `python manage.py runserver` again you should no longer see any warnings.

HTTP Request/Response Cycle

HTTP (Hypertext Transfer Protocol)[20] was initially created by Tim Berners-Lee in 1989 and is the foundation of the World Wide Web. A network protocol is a set of rules for formatting and processing data. It is like a common language for computers that allows them to communicate with one another even if they are located on opposite sides of the earth and have vastly different hardware and software.

HTTP is a request-response protocol that works in a client-server computing model. Every time you visit a webpage an initial "request" is sent by the "client" (ie your computer) and a "response" is sent back by a "server." The client doesn't have to be a computer though, it could also be a mobile phone or any internet-connected device. But the process is the same: an HTTP request is sent to a URL by a client and a server sends back an HTTP response.

Ultimately, all a web framework like Django does is accept HTTP requests to a given URL and return a HTTP response containing the information necessary to render a webpage. That's it. Generally this process involves identifying the proper URL, connecting to a database, adding some logic, applying style with HTML/CSS/JavaScript/static assets, and then return the HTTP response. That's it.

The abstract flow looks something like this:

---

[20]https://en.wikipedia.org/wiki/Hypertext_Transfer_Protocol

Web Framework

```
HTTP Request -> URL -> Django combines database, logic, styling -> HTTP Response
```

Model-View-Controller vs Model-View-Template

Over time the **Model-View-Controller (MVC)** pattern has emerged as a popular way to *internally* separate the data, logic, and display of an application into separate components. This makes it easier for a developer to reason about the code. The MVC pattern is widely used among web frameworks including Ruby on Rails, Spring (Java), Laravel (PHP), ASP.NET (C#) and many others.

In the traditional MVC pattern there are three major components:

- Model: Manages data and core business logic
- View: Renders data from the model in a particular format
- Controller: Accepts user input and performs application-specific logic

Django only loosely follows the traditional MVC approach with its own version often called **Model-View-Template (MVT)**. This can be initially confusing to developers with previous web framework experience. In reality, Django's approach is really it is a 4-part pattern that also incorporates URL Configuration so something like MVTU would be a more accurate description.

The Django MVT pattern is as follows:

- Model: Manages data and core business logic
- View: Describes *which* data is sent to the user but not its presentation
- Template: Presents the data as HTML with optional CSS, JavaScript, and Static Assets
- URL Configuration: Regular-expression components configured to a View

This interaction is fundamental to Django yet **very confusing** to newcomers so let's map out the order of a given HTTP request/response cycle. When you type in a URL, such as `https://djangoproject.com`, the first thing that happens within our Django project is a URL pattern (contained in `urls.py`) is found that matches it. The URL pattern is linked to a single view (contained in `views.py`) which combines the data from the model (stored in `models.py`) and the styling from a template (any file ending in `.html`). The view then returns a HTTP response to the user.

The complete Django flow looks like this:

Django request/response cycle

```
HTTP Request -> URL -> View -> Model and Template -> HTTP Response
```

If you are brand new to web development the distinction between MVC and MVT will not matter much. This book demonstrates the Django way of doing things so there won't be confusion. However if you are a web developer with previous MVC experience, it can take a little while to shift your thinking to the "Django way" of doing things which is more loosely coupled and allows for easier modifications.

Create An App

Django uses the concept of projects and apps to keep code clean and readable. A single top-level Django project can contain multiple apps. Each app controls an isolated piece of functionality. For example, an e-commerce site might have one app for user authentication, another app for payments, and a third app to power item listing details. That's three distinct apps that all live within one top-level project. How and when you split functionality into apps is somewhat subjective, but in general, each app should have a clear function.

To add a new app go to the command line and quit the running server with `Control+c`. Then use the `startapp` command followed by the name of our app which will be `pages`.

Shell

```
# Windows
(.venv) > python manage.py startapp pages

# macOS
(.venv) % python3 manage.py startapp pages
```

If you look visually at the `helloworld` directory Django has created within it a new `pages` directory containing the following files:

Code

```
├── pages
│   ├── __init__.py
│   ├── admin.py
│   ├── apps.py
│   ├── migrations
│   │   └── __init__.py
│   ├── models.py
│   ├── tests.py
│   └── views.py
```

Let's review what each new `pages` app file does:

- `admin.py` is a configuration file for the built-in Django Admin app
- `apps.py` is a configuration file for the app itself
- `migrations/` keeps track of any changes to our `models.py` file so it stays in sync with our database
- `models.py` is where we define our database models which Django automatically translates into database tables
- `tests.py` is for app-specific tests
- `views.py` is where we handle the request/response logic for our web app

Notice that the model, view, and url from the MVT pattern are present from the beginning. The only thing missing is a template which we'll add shortly.

Even though our new app exists within the Django project, Django doesn't "know" about it until we explicitly add it to the `django_project/settings.py` file. In your text editor open the file up and scroll down to INSTALLED_APPS where you'll see six built-in Django apps already there. Add pages.apps.PagesConfig at the bottom.

Code

```
# django_project/settings.py
INSTALLED_APPS = [
    "django.contrib.admin",
    "django.contrib.auth",
    "django.contrib.contenttypes",
    "django.contrib.sessions",
    "django.contrib.messages",
    "django.contrib.staticfiles",
    "pages.apps.PagesConfig",  # new
]
```

If you have Black installed in your text editor on "save" it will change all the single quotes '' here to double quotes "". That's fine. As noted previously, Django has plans to adopt Black Python formatting fully in the future.

What is PagesConfig you might ask? Well, it is the name of the solitary function within the pages/apps.py file at this point.

Code

```
# pages/apps.py
from django.apps import AppConfig


class PagesConfig(AppConfig):
    default_auto_field = "django.db.models.BigAutoField"
    name = "pages"
```

Don't worry if you are confused at this point: it takes practice to internalize how Django projects and apps are structured. Over the course of this book we will build many projects and apps and the patterns will soon become familiar.

Hello, World

In Django, four separate files aligning with this MVT pattern are required to power one single dynamic (aka linked to a database) webpage:

- `models.py`
- `views.py`
- `template.html` (any HTML file will do)
- `urls.py`

However, to create a static webpage (not linked to a database) we can hardcode the data into a view so the model is not needed. That's what we'll do here to keep things simple. From Chapter 4 onwards we'll be using the model in all our projects.

The next step is therefore to create our first view. Start by updating the `views.py` file in our `pages` app to look as follows:

Code

```
# pages/views.py
from django.http import HttpResponse


def homePageView(request):
    return HttpResponse("Hello, World!")
```

Basically, we're saying whenever the view function `homePageView` is called, return the text "Hello, World!" More specifically, we've imported the built-in HttpResponse[21] method so we can return a response object to the user. We've created a function called `homePageView` that accepts the `request` object and returns a `response` with the string "Hello, World!"

There are two types of views in Django: function-based views (FBVs) and class-based views (CBVs). Our code in this example is a function-based view: it is relatively simple to implement and explicit. Django originally started with only FBVs but over time added CBVs which allow for much greater code reusability, keeps things DRY (Don't-Repeat-Yourself), and can be extended via mixins. The additional abstraction of CBVs makes them quite powerful and concise, however it also makes them harder to read for Django newcomers.

Because web development quickly becomes repetitive Django also comes with a number of built-in generic class-based views (GCBVs) to handle common use cases such as creating a new object,

---

[21]https://docs.djangoproject.com/en/4.0/ref/request-response/#django.http.HttpResponse

forms, list views, pagination, and so on. We will be using GCBVs heavily in this book in later chapters.

There are therefore technically three ways to write a view in Django: function-based views (FBVs), class-based views (CBVs), and generic class-based views (GCBVs). This customization is helpful for advanced developers but confusing for newcomers. Many Django developers–including your author–prefer to use GCBVs when possible and revert to CBVs or FBVs when required. By the end of this book you will have used all three and can make up your own mind on which approach you prefer.

Moving along we need to configure our URLs. In your text editor, create a new file called urls.py within the pages app. Then update it with the following code:

Code

```
# pages/urls.py
from django.urls import path
from .views import homePageView

urlpatterns = [
    path("", homePageView, name="home"),
]
```

On the top line we import path from Django to power our URL pattern and on the next line we import our views. By referring to the views.py file as .views we are telling Django to look within the current directory for a views.py file and import the view homePageView from there.

Our URL pattern has three parts:

- a Python regular expression for the empty string ""
- a reference to the view called homePageView
- an optional named URL pattern[22] called "home"

In other words, if the user requests the homepage represented by the empty string "", Django should use the view called homePageView.

---

[22]https://docs.djangoproject.com/en/4.0/topics/http/urls/#naming-url-patterns

We're *almost* done at this point. The last step is to update our `django_project/urls.py` file. It's common to have multiple apps within a single Django project, like `pages` here, and they each need their own dedicated URL path.

Code

```
# django_project/urls.py
from django.contrib import admin
from django.urls import path, include  # new

urlpatterns = [
    path("admin/", admin.site.urls),
    path("", include("pages.urls")),  # new
]
```

We've imported `include` on the second line next to `path` and then created a new URL pattern for our `pages` app. Now whenever a user visits the homepage, they will first be routed to the `pages` app and then to the `homePageView` view set in the `pages/urls.py` file.

This need for two separate `urls.py` files is often confusing to beginners. Think of the top-level `django_project/urls.py` as the gateway to various url patterns distinct to each app.

We have all the code we need now. To confirm everything works as expected, restart our Django server:

Shell

```
# Windows
(.venv) > python manage.py runserver

# macOS
(.venv) % python3 manage.py runserver
```

If you refresh the browser for `http://127.0.0.1:8000/` it now displays the text "Hello, World!"

Hello World homepage

Git

In the previous chapter we installed the version control system Git. Let's use it here. The first step is to initialize (or add) Git to our repository. Make sure you've stopped the local server with `Control+c`, then run the command `git init`.

Shell

```
(.venv) > git init
```

If you then type `git status` you'll see a list of changes since the last Git commit. Since this is our first commit, this list is all of our changes so far.

Shell

```
(.venv) > git status
On branch main

No commits yet

Untracked files:
  (use "git add <file>..." to include in what will be committed)

        .venv
        django_project/
        db.sqlite3
        manage.py
        pages/

nothing added to commit but untracked files present (use "git add" to track)
```

Note that our virtual environment `.venv` is included which is *not* a best practice. It should be kept out of Git source control since secret information such as API keys and the like are often included in it. The solution is to create a new file called `.gitignore` which tells Git what to ignore. The period at the beginning indicates this is a "hidden" file. The file still exists but it is a way to communicate to developers that the contents are probably meant for configuration and not source control. In this new file, add a single line for `.venv`.

.gitignore

```
.venv/
```

If you run `git status` again you will see that `.venv` is not longer there. It has been "ignored" by Git.

At the same time, we *do* want a record of packages installed in our virtual environment. The current best practice is to create a `requirements.txt` file with this information. The command `pip freeze` will output the contents of your current virtual environment and by using the > operator we can do all this in one step: output the contents into a new file called `requirements.txt`. If your server is still running enter `Ctrl+c` and `Enter` to exit before entering this command.

Shell

```
(.venv) > pip freeze > requirements.txt
```

A new `requirements.txt` file will appear with all our installed packages and their dependencies. If you look *inside* this file you'll see there are actually four packages even though we have installed only one.

requirements.txt

```
asgiref==3.4.1
Django==4.0
sqlparse==0.4.2
```

That's because Django relies on *other* packages for support, too. It is often the case that when you install one Python package you're often installing several others it depends on as well. Since it is difficult to keep track of all the packages a `requirements.txt` file is very important.

We next want to add *all* recent changes by using the command `add -A` and then `commit` the changes along with a message (`-m`) describing what has changed.

Shell

```
(.venv) > git add -A
(.venv) > git commit -m "initial commit"
```

In professional projects a .gitignore file is typically quite lengthy. For efficiency and security reasons, there are often quite a few directories and files that should be removed from source control. We will cover this more thoroughly in Chapter 16 when we do a professional-grade deployment.

GitHub

It's a good habit to create a remote repository of your code for each project. This way you have a backup in case anything happens to your computer and more importantly, it allows for collaboration with other software developers. Popular choices include GitHub, Bitbucket, and GitLab. When you're learning web development, it's best to stick to private rather than public repositories so you don't inadvertently post critical information such as passwords online.

We will use GitHub in this book but all three services offer similar functionality for newcomers. Sign up for a free account on GitHub's homepage and verify your email address. Then navigate to the "Create a new repository" page located at https://github.com/new[23].

Enter the repository name hello-world and click on the radio button next to "Private" rather than "Public." Then click on the button at the bottom for "Create Repository."

Your first repository is now created! However there is no code in it yet. Scroll down on the page to where it says "...or push an existing repository from the command line." That's what we want. Copy the text immediately under this headline and paste it into your command line. Here is what it looks like for me with my GitHub username of wsvincent. Your username will be different.

---

[23]https://github.com/new

Shell

```
> git remote add origin https://github.com/wsvincent/hello-world.git
> git branch -M main
> git push -u origin main
```

The first line syncs the local directory on our computer with the remote repository on the GitHub website. The next line establishes the default branch as `main` which is what we want. And then the third line "pushes" the code up to GitHub's servers.

Assuming everything worked properly, you can now go back to your GitHub webpage and refresh it. Your local code is now hosted online!

SSH Keys

Unfortunately, there is a good chance that the last command yielded an error if you are a new developer and do not have SSH keys already configured.

Shell

```
ERROR: Repository not found.
fatal: Could not read from remote repository.

Please make sure you have the correct access rights
and the repository exists.
```

This cryptic message means we need to configure SSH keys. This is a one-time thing but a bit of a hassle to be honest.

SSH is a protocol used to ensure private connections with a remote server. Think of it as an additional layer of privacy on top of username/password. The process involves generating unique SSH keys and storing them on your computer so only GitHub can access them.

First, check whether you have existing SSH keys. Github has a guide to this[24] that works for Mac, Windows, and Linux. If you *don't* have existing public and private keys, you'll need to generate them. GitHub, again, has a guide on doing this[25].

---

[24]https://help.github.com/en/articles/checking-for-existing-ssh-keys
[25]https://help.github.com/en/articles/generating-a-new-ssh-key-and-adding-it-to-the-ssh-agent

Once complete you should be able to execute the `git push -u origin main` command successfully!

It's normal to feel overwhelmed and frustrated if you become stuck with SSH keys. GitHub has a lot of resources to walk you through it but the reality is its very intimidating the first time. If you're truly stuck, continue with the book and come back to SSH Keys and GitHub with a full nights sleep. I can't count the number of times a clear head has helped me process a difficult programming issue.

Assuming success with GitHub, go ahead and exit our virtual environment with the `deactivate` command.

Shell

```
(.venv) > deactivate
```

You should no longer see parentheses on your command line, indicating the virtual environment is no longer active.

Conclusion

Congratulations! We've covered a lot of fundamental concepts in this chapter. We built our first Django application and learned about Django's project/app structure. We started to learn about views, urls, and the internal Django web server. And we worked with Git to track our changes and pushed our code into a private repo on GitHub.

If you became stuck at any point make sure to compare your code against the official repo[26].

Continue on to **Chapter 3: Pages app** where we'll build and deploy a more complex Django application using templates and class-based views.

---

[26]https://github.com/wsvincent/djangoforbeginners

Chapter 3: Pages App

In this chapter we will build, test, and deploy a *Pages* app containing a homepage and about page. We still aren't touching the database yet–that comes in the next chapter–but we'll learn about class-based views and templates which are the building blocks for the more complex web applications built later on in the book.

Initial Set Up

As in **Chapter 2: Hello World App**, our initial set up involves the following steps:

- make a new directory for our code called `pages` and navigate into it
- create a new virtual environment called `.venv` and activate it
- install Django
- create a new Django project called `django_project`
- create a new app called `pages`

On the command line make sure you're not working in an existing virtual environment. If there is text before the command line prompt–either > on Windows or % on macOS–then you are! Make sure to type `deactivate` to leave it.

Within a new command line shell start by typing the following:

Shell

```
# Windows
> cd onedrive\desktop\code
> mkdir pages
> cd pages
> python -m venv .venv
> .venv\Scripts\Activate.ps1
(.venv) > python -m pip install django~=4.0.0
(.venv) > django-admin startproject django_project .
(.venv) > python manage.py startapp pages

# macOS
% cd ~/desktop/code
% mkdir pages
% cd pages
% python3 -m venv .venv
% source .venv/bin/activate
(.venv) % python3 -m pip install django~=4.0.0
(.venv) % django-admin startproject django_project .
(.venv) % python3 manage.py startapp pages
```

Remember that even though we added a new app, Django will not recognize it until it is added
to the INSTALLED_APPS setting within django_project/settings.py. Open your text editor and
add it to the bottom now:

Code

```
# django_project/settings.py
INSTALLED_APPS = [
    "django.contrib.admin",
    "django.contrib.auth",
    "django.contrib.contenttypes",
    "django.contrib.sessions",
    "django.contrib.messages",
    "django.contrib.staticfiles",
    "pages.apps.PagesConfig",  # new
]
```

Migrate the database with migrate and start the local web server with runserver.

Shell

```
(.venv) > python manage.py migrate
(.venv) > python manage.py runserver
```

And then navigate to `http://127.0.0.1:8000/`.

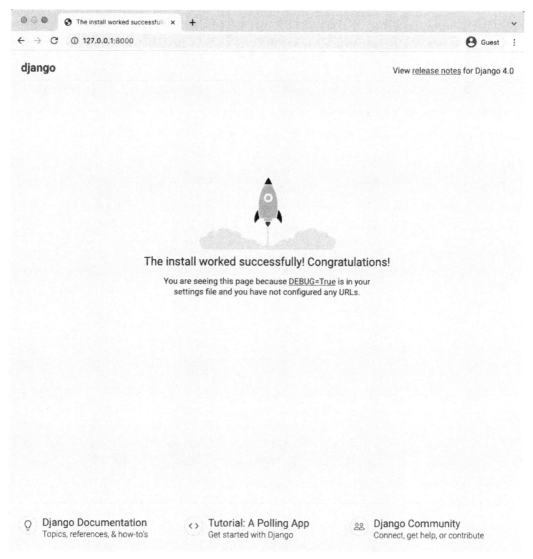

Django welcome page

Templates

Every web framework needs a convenient way to generate HTML files and in Django the approach is to use *templates*: individual HTML files that can be linked together and also include basic logic.

Recall that in the previous chapter our "Hello, World" site had the phrase hardcoded into a `views.py` file. That technically works but doesn't scale well! A better approach is to link a view to a template, thereby separating the information contained in each.

In this chapter we'll learn how to use templates to more easily create our desired homepage and about page. And in future chapters, the use of templates will support building websites that can support hundreds, thousands, or even millions of webpages with a minimal amount of code.

The first consideration is where to place templates within the structure of a Django project. There are two options. By default, Django's template loader will look within each app for related templates. However the structure is somewhat confusing: each app needs a new `templates` directory, another directory with the same name as the app, and then the template file.

Therefore, in our `pages` app, Django would expect the following layout:

Layout

```
└── pages
    ├── templates
        ├── pages
            ├── home.html
```

This means we would need to create a new `templates` directory, a new directory with the name of the app, `pages`, and finally our template itself which is `home.html`.

Why this seemingly repetitive approach? The short answer is that the Django template loader wants to be really sure it finds the correct template! What happens if there are `home.html` files within two separate apps? This structure makes sure there are no such conflicts.

There is, however, another approach which is to instead create a single project-level `templates` directory and place *all* templates within there. By making a small tweak to our `django_-project/settings.py` file we can tell Django to *also* look in this directory for templates. That is the approach we'll use.

First, quit the running server with the `Control+c` command. Then create a directory called `templates`.

Shell

```
(.venv) > mkdir templates
```

Next we need to update `django_project/settings.py` to tell Django the location of our new `templates` directory. This is a one-line change to the setting `"DIRS"` under `TEMPLATES`.

Code

```
# django_project/settings.py
TEMPLATES = [
    {
        ...
        "DIRS": [BASE_DIR / "templates"],  # new
        ...
    },
]
```

Within the `templates` directory create a new file called `home.html`. You can do this within your text editor: in Visual Studio Code go to the top left of your screen, click on "File" and then "New File." Make sure to name and save the file in the correct location.

The `home.html` file will have a simple headline for now.

Code

```
<!-- templates/home.html -->
<h1>Homepage</h1>
```

Ok, our template is complete! The next step is to configure our URL and view files.

Class-Based Views

Early versions of Django only shipped with function-based views, but developers soon found themselves repeating the same patterns over and over again. Write a view that lists all objects in a model. Write a view that displays only one detailed item from a model. And so on.

Function-based generic views were introduced to abstract these patterns and streamline development of common patterns. However, there was no easy way to extend or customize these views[27]. As a result, Django introduced class-based generic views that make it easy to use and also extend views covering common use cases.

Classes are a fundamental part of Python but a thorough discussion of them is beyond the scope of this book. If you need an introduction or refresher, I suggest reviewing the official Python docs[28] which have an excellent tutorial on classes and their usage.

In our view we will use the built-in TemplateView[29] to display our template. Update the pages/views.py file.

Code

```
# pages/views.py
from django.views.generic import TemplateView


class HomePageView(TemplateView):
    template_name = "home.html"
```

Note that we've capitalized our view, HomePageView, since it's now a Python class. Classes, unlike functions, should always be capitalized[30]. The TemplateView already contains all the logic needed to display our template, we just need to specify the template's name.

URLs

The last step is to update our URLs. Recall from Chapter 2 that we need to make updates in two locations. First, we update the django_project/urls.py file to point at our pages app and then within pages we match views to URL routes.

Let's start with the django_project/urls.py file.

---

[27]https://docs.djangoproject.com/en/4.0/topics/class-based-views/intro/

[28]https://docs.python.org/3.10/tutorial/classes.html

[29]https://docs.djangoproject.com/en/4.0/ref/class-based-views/base/#django.views.generic.base. TemplateView

[30]https://www.python.org/dev/peps/pep-0008/#class-names

Code

```
# django_project/urls.py
from django.contrib import admin
from django.urls import path, include  # new

urlpatterns = [
    path("admin/", admin.site.urls),
    path("", include("pages.urls")),  # new
]
```

The code here should look familiar at this point. We add `include` on the second line to point the existing URL to the `pages` app. Next create a file called `pages/urls.py` file and add the code below. This pattern is almost identical to what we did in Chapter 2 with one major difference: when using Class-Based Views, you always add `as_view()` at the end of the view name.

Code

```
# pages/urls.py
from django.urls import path
from .views import HomePageView

urlpatterns = [
    path("", HomePageView.as_view(), name="home"),
]
```

And we're done! Start up the local web server with the command `python manage.py runserver` and navigate to `http://127.0.0.1:8000/` to see our new homepage.

Homepage

About Page

The process for adding an about page is very similar to what we just did. We'll create a new template file, a new view, and a new url route. Start by making a new template file called templates/about.html and populate it with a short HTML headline.

Code

```
<!-- templates/about.html -->
<h1>About page</h1>
```

Then add a new view for the page.

Code

```
# pages/views.py
from django.views.generic import TemplateView


class HomePageView(TemplateView):
    template_name = "home.html"


class AboutPageView(TemplateView):  # new
    template_name = "about.html"
```

And finally import the view name and connect it to a URL at about/.

Code

```
# pages/urls.py
from django.urls import path
from .views import HomePageView, AboutPageView  # new

urlpatterns = [
    path("about/", AboutPageView.as_view(), name="about"),  # new
    path("", HomePageView.as_view(), name="home"),
]
```

Start up the web server with runserver and navigate to http://127.0.0.1:8000/about. The new About page is visible.

About page

Extending Templates

The real power of templates is their ability to be extended. If you think about most websites, there is content that is repeated on every page (header, footer, etc). Wouldn't it be nice if we, as developers, could have *one canonical place* for our header code that would be inherited by all other templates?

Well we can! Let's create a `base.html` file containing a header with links to our two pages. We could name this file anything but using `base.html` is a common convention. In your text editor make this new file called `templates/base.html`.

Django has a minimal templating language for adding links and basic logic in our templates. You can see the full list of built-in template tags here in the official docs[31]. Template tags take the form of `{% something %}` where the "something" is the template tag itself. You can even create your own custom template tags, though we won't do that in this book.

To add URL links in our project we can use the built-in url template tag[32] which takes the URL pattern name as an argument. Remember how we added optional URL names to our two routes in `pages/urls.py`? This is why. The `url` tag uses these names to automatically create links for us.

The URL route for our homepage is called `home`. To configure a link to it we use the following syntax: `{% url 'home' %}`.

---

[31]https://docs.djangoproject.com/en/4.0/ref/templates/builtins/#built-in-template-tags-and-filters
[32]https://docs.djangoproject.com/en/4.0/ref/templates/builtins/#url

Code

```
<!-- templates/base.html -->
<header>
  <a href="{% url 'home' %}">Home</a> |
  <a href="{% url 'about' %}">About</a>
</header>

{% block content %} {% endblock content %}
```

At the bottom we've added a `block` tag called `content`. Blocks can be overwritten by child templates via inheritance. While it's optional to name our closing `endblock`–you can just write `{% endblock %}` if you prefer–doing so helps with readability, especially in larger template files.

Let's update our `home.html` and `about.html` files to extend the `base.html` template. That means we can reuse the same code from one template in another template. The Django templating language comes with an extends[33] method that we can use for this.

Code

```
<!-- templates/home.html -->
{% extends "base.html" %}

{% block content %}
<h1>Homepage</h1>
{% endblock content %}
```

Code

```
<!-- templates/about.html -->
{% extends "base.html" %}

{% block content %}
<h1>About page</h1>
{% endblock content %}
```

Now if you start up the server with `python manage.py runserver` and open up our webpages again at `http://127.0.0.1:8000/` the header is included.

---

[33]https://docs.djangoproject.com/en/4.0/ref/templates/builtins/#extends

Homepage with header

And it is also present on the about page at `http://127.0.0.1:8000/about`.

About page with header

There's *a lot* more we can do with templates and in practice you'll typically create a `base.html` file and then add additional templates on top of it in a robust Django project. We'll do this later on in the book.

Tests

It's important to add automated tests and run them whenever a codebase changes. Tests require a small amount of upfront time to write but more than pay off later on. In the words of Django co-creator Jacob Kaplan-Moss[34], "Code without tests is broken as designed."

Testing can be divided into two main categories: unit and integration. *Unit tests* check a piece of functionality in isolation, while *Integration tests* check multiple pieces linked together. Unit tests run faster and are easier to maintain since they focus on only a small piece of code. Integration tests are slower and harder to maintain since a failure doesn't point you in the specific direction of the cause. Most developers focus on writing many unit tests and a small amount of integration tests.

---

[34]https://jacobian.org/

The Python standard library contains a built-in testing framework called unittest[35] that uses TestCase[36] instances and a long list of assert methods[37] to check for and report failures.

Django's own testing framework provides several extensions on top of Python's unittest.TestCase base class. These include a test client[38] for making dummy Web browser requests, a number of Django-specific additional assertions[39], and four test case classes: SimpleTestCase[40], TestCase[41], TransactionTestCase[42], and LiveServerTestCase[43].

Generally speaking, SimpleTestCase is used when a database is not necessary while TestCase is used when you do want to test the database. TransactionTestCase is useful if you need to directly test database transactions[44] while LiveServerTestCase launches a live server thread useful for testing with browser-based tools like Selenium.

One quick note before we proceed: you may notice that the *naming* of methods in unittest and django.test are written in camelCase rather than the more Pythonic snake_case pattern. The reason is that unittest is based on the jUnit testing framework from Java, which does use camelCase, so when unittest was added to Python it came along with camelCase naming.

If you look within our pages app, Django already provided a tests.py file we can use. Since no database is involved yet in our project we will import SimpleTestCase at the top of the file. For our first tests we'll check that the two URLs for our website, the homepage and about page, both return HTTP status codes[45] of 200, the standard response for a successful HTTP request.

---

[35] https://docs.python.org/3/library/unittest.html
[36] https://docs.python.org/3/library/unittest.html#unittest.TestCase
[37] https://docs.python.org/3/library/unittest.html#assert-methods
[38] https://docs.djangoproject.com/en/4.0/topics/testing/tools/#the-test-client
[39] https://docs.djangoproject.com/en/4.0/topics/testing/tools/#assertions
[40] https://docs.djangoproject.com/en/4.0/topics/testing/tools/#simpletestcase
[41] https://docs.djangoproject.com/en/4.0/topics/testing/tools/#testcase
[42] https://docs.djangoproject.com/en/4.0/topics/testing/tools/#transactiontestcase
[43] https://docs.djangoproject.com/en/4.0/topics/testing/tools/#django.test.LiveServerTestCase
[44] https://docs.djangoproject.com/en/4.0/topics/db/transactions/
[45] https://en.wikipedia.org/wiki/List_of_HTTP_status_codes

Code

```
# pages/tests.py
from django.test import SimpleTestCase


class HomepageTests(SimpleTestCase):
    def test_url_exists_at_correct_location(self):
        response = self.client.get("/")
        self.assertEqual(response.status_code, 200)


class AboutpageTests(SimpleTestCase):
    def test_url_exists_at_correct_location(self):
        response = self.client.get("/about/")
        self.assertEqual(response.status_code, 200)
```

To run the tests quit the server with `Control+c` and type `python manage.py test` on the command line to run the tests.

Shell

```
(.venv) > python manage.py test
System check identified no issues (0 silenced).
..
----------------------------------------------------------------------
Ran 2 tests in 0.006s

OK
```

If you see an error such as `AssertionError: 301 != 200` it's likely you forgot to add the trailing slash to `"/about"` above. The web browser knows to automatically add a slash if it's not provided, but that causes a 301 redirect, not a 200 success response!

What else can we test? How about the URL name for each page? Recall that in `pages/urls.py` we added the name of `"home"` for the homepage path and `"about"` for the about page. We can use the very handy Django utility function reverse[46] to check both. Make sure to import `reverse` at the top of the file and add a new unit test for each below.

---

[46]https://docs.djangoproject.com/en/4.0/ref/urlresolvers/#reverse

Code

```
# pages/tests.py
from django.test import SimpleTestCase
from django.urls import reverse  # new


class HomepageTests(SimpleTestCase):
    def test_url_exists_at_correct_location(self):
        response = self.client.get("/")
        self.assertEqual(response.status_code, 200)

    def test_url_available_by_name(self):  # new
        response = self.client.get(reverse("home"))
        self.assertEqual(response.status_code, 200)


class AboutpageTests(SimpleTestCase):
    def test_url_exists_at_correct_location(self):
        response = self.client.get("/about/")
        self.assertEqual(response.status_code, 200)

    def test_url_available_by_name(self):  # new
        response = self.client.get(reverse("about"))
        self.assertEqual(response.status_code, 200)
```

Run the tests again to confirm that they work correctly.

Shell

```
(.venv) > python manage.py test
System check identified no issues (0 silenced).
..
----------------------------------------------------------------
Ran 4 tests in 0.007s

OK
```

We have tested our URL locations and URL names so far but not our templates. Let's make sure that the correct templates–`home.html` and `about.html`–are used on each page and that they display the expected content of "<h1>Homepage</h1>" and "<h1>About page</h1>" respectively.

We can use assertTemplateUsed[47] and assertContains[48] to achieve this.

Code

```
# pages/tests.py
from django.test import SimpleTestCase
from django.urls import reverse


class HomepageTests(SimpleTestCase):
    def test_url_exists_at_correct_location(self):
        response = self.client.get("/")
        self.assertEqual(response.status_code, 200)

    def test_url_available_by_name(self):
        response = self.client.get(reverse("home"))
        self.assertEqual(response.status_code, 200)

    def test_template_name_correct(self):  # new
        response = self.client.get(reverse("home"))
        self.assertTemplateUsed(response, "home.html")

    def test_template_content(self):  # new
        response = self.client.get(reverse("home"))
        self.assertContains(response, "<h1>Homepage</h1>")


class AboutpageTests(SimpleTestCase):
    def test_url_exists_at_correct_location(self):
        response = self.client.get("/about/")
        self.assertEqual(response.status_code, 200)

    def test_url_available_by_name(self):
        response = self.client.get(reverse("about"))
        self.assertEqual(response.status_code, 200)

    def test_template_name_correct(self):  # new
        response = self.client.get(reverse("about"))
        self.assertTemplateUsed(response, "about.html")

    def test_template_content(self):  # new
```

---

[47]https://docs.djangoproject.com/en/4.0/topics/testing/tools/#django.test.SimpleTestCase.
assertTemplateUsed

[48]https://docs.djangoproject.com/en/4.0/topics/testing/tools/#django.test.SimpleTestCase.assertContains

```
                response = self.client.get(reverse("about"))
                self.assertContains(response, "<h1>About page</h1>")
```

Run the tests one last time to check our new work. Everything should pass.

Shell

```
(.venv) > python manage.py test
System check identified no issues (0 silenced).
..
----------------------------------------------------------------
Ran 8 tests in 0.009s

OK
```

Experienced programmers may look at our testing code and note that there is a lot of repetition. For example, we are setting the `response` each time for all eight tests. Generally it is a good idea to abide by the concept of DRY (Don't Repeat Yourself) coding, but unit tests work best when they are self contained and extremely verbose. As a test suite expands, for performance reasons it might make more sense to combine multiple assertions into a smaller number of test but that is an advanced–and often subjective-topic beyond the scope of this book.

We'll do much more with testing in the future, especially once we start working with databases. For now, it's important to see how easy and important it is to add tests each and every time we add new functionality to our Django project.

Git and GitHub

It's time to track our changes with Git and push them up to GitHub. We'll start by initializing our directory and checking the status of our changes.

Shell

```
(.venv) > git init
(.venv) > git status
```

Use `git status` to see all our code changes. Notice that the `.venv` directory with our virtual environment is included? We don't want that. In your text editor create a new hidden file, `.gitignore`, so we can specify what Git will *not* track.

.gitignore

```
.venv/
```

Run `git status` again to confirm these two files are being ignored, then use `git add -A` to add the intended files/directories, and finally add an initial commit message.

Shell

```
(.venv) > git status
(.venv) > git add -A
(.venv) > git commit -m "initial commit"
```

Over on GitHub create a new repo[49] called `pages` and make sure to select the "Private" radio button. Then click on the "Create repository" button.

On the next page, scroll down to where it says "...or push an existing repository from the command line." Copy and paste the two commands there into your terminal.

It should look like the below albeit instead of `wsvincent` as the username it will be your GitHub username.

Shell

```
(.venv) > git remote add origin https://github.com/wsvincent/pages.git
(.venv) > git push -u origin main
```

---

[49]https://github.com/new

Local vs Production

To make our site available on the Internet where everyone can see it, we need to deploy our code
to an external server and database. This is called putting our code into *production*. Local code
lives only on our computer; production code lives on an external server available to everyone.

The `startproject` command creates a new project configured for local development via the
file `django_project/settings.py`. This ease-of-use means when it does come time to push the
project into production, a number of settings have to be changed.

One of these is the web server. Django comes with its own basic server, suitable for local usage,
but it *is not* suitable for production. There are two options available: Gunicorn[50] and uWSGI[51].
Gunicorn is the simpler to configure and more than adequate for our projects so that will be
what we use.

For our hosting provider we will use Heroku[52] because it is free for small projects, widely-used,
and has a relatively straightforward deployment process.

Heroku

You can sign up for a free Heroku account on their website. Fill in the registration form and wait
for an email with a link to confirm your account. This will take you to the password setup page.
Once configured, you will be directed to the dashboard section of the site. Heroku now requires
enrolling in multi-factor authentication (MFA), too, which can be done with SalesForce or a tool
like Google Authenticator.

Heroku may also ask about adding a credit card for account verification[53]. This is optional but
provides extra benefits even if you use the free tier such as adding a custom domain and adding
extra add-ons for additional functionality.

Now that you are signed up, it is time to install Heroku's *Command Line Interface* (CLI) so we
can deploy from the command line. Currently, we are operating within a virtual environment

---

[50]http://gunicorn.org/
[51]https://uwsgi-docs.readthedocs.io/en/latest/
[52]https://www.heroku.com/
[53]https://devcenter.heroku.com/articles/account-verification

for our *Pages* project but we want Heroku available globally, that is everywhere on our machine. An easy way to do so is open up a new command line tab–Command+t on a Mac, Control+t on Windows–which is not operating in a virtual environment. Anything installed here will be global.

On Windows, see the Heroku CLI page[54] to correctly install either the 32-bit or 64-bit version. On a Mac, the package manager Homebrew[55] is used for installation. If not already on your machine, install Homebrew by copy and pasting the long command on the Homebrew website into your command line and hitting Return. It will look something like this:

Shell

```
% /bin/bash -c "$(curl -fsSL https://raw.githubusercontent.com/Homebrew/\
  install/HEAD/install.sh)"
```

Next install the Heroku CLI by copy and pasting the following into your command line and hitting Return.

Shell

```
% brew tap heroku/brew && brew install heroku
```

If you are on a new M1 chip Apple computer you might receive an error with something like Bad CPU type in executable. Installing Rosetta 2[56] will solve the issue.

Once installation is complete you can close the new command line tab and return to the initial tab with the pages virtual environment active.

Type the command heroku login and use the email and password for Heroku you just set.

---

[54]https://devcenter.heroku.com/articles/heroku-cli#download-and-install
[55]https://brew.sh/
[56]https://support.apple.com/en-us/HT211861

Shell

```
(.venv) > heroku login
Enter your Heroku credentials:
Email: will@wsvincent.com
Password: ********************************
Logged in as will@wsvincent.com
```

You are logged in and ready to go!

Deployment Checklist

Deployment typically requires a number of discrete steps. It is common to have a "checklist" for these since there quickly become too many to remember. At this stage, we are intentionally keeping things basic however this list will grow in future projects as we add additional security and performance features.

Here is the current deployment checklist:

- install `Gunicorn`
- create a `requirements.txt` file
- update `ALLOWED_HOSTS` in `django_project/settings.py`
- create a `Procfile`
- create a `runtime.txt` file

The first item is to install Gunicorn, a production-ready web server for our project. Recall that we have been using Django's own lightweight server for development purposes but it is not suitable for a live website. Gunicorn can be installed using Pip.

Shell

```
(.venv) > python -m pip install gunicorn==20.1.0
```

Step two is to create a `requirements.txt` file containing all the specific Python dependencies in our project. That is, every Python package currently installed in our virtual environment. This is necessary in case we–or a team member–want to recreate the repository from scratch in the future. It also helps Heroku recognize that this is a Python project, which simplifies the deployment steps.

To create this file, we will redirect the output of the `pip freeze` command to a new file called `requirements.txt`.

Shell

```
(.venv) > python -m pip freeze > requirements.txt
```

If you look at the contents of this file it contains `Django`, `gunicorn`, `asgiref` and `sqlparse`. That's because when we installed Django we *also* end up installing a number of other Python modules it depends upon. You do not need to focus too much on the contents of this file, just remember that whenever you install a new Python package in your virtual environment you should update the `requirements.txt` file to reflect it. There are more complicated tools that automate this process but since we are using `venv` and keeping things as simple as possible, it must be done manually.

The third step is to look within `django_project/settings.py` for the ALLOWED_HOSTS[57] setting, which represents that host/domain names our Django site can serve. This is a security measure to prevent HTTP Host header attacks. For now, we'll use the wildcard asterisk, `*` so that *all* domains are acceptable. Later in the book we'll see how to explicitly list the domains that should be allowed which is much more secure.

Code

```
# django_project/settings.py
ALLOWED_HOSTS = ["*"]
```

The fourth step is to create a new `Procfile` in the base directory next to the `manage.py` file. The `Procfile` is specific to Heroku and provides instructions on how to run the application in their stack. We're indicating that for the `web` function use `gunicorn` as the server, the WSGI config file located at `django_project.wsgi`, and finally the flag `--log-file` - makes any logging messages visible to us.

---

[57]https://docs.djangoproject.com/en/4.0/ref/settings/#allowed-hosts

Procfile

```
web: gunicorn django_project.wsgi --log-file -
```

The final step is to specify which Python version should run on Heroku. If not set explicitly this is currently set[58] to the `python-3.9.10` runtime but changes over time. Since we are using Python 3.10 we must create a dedicated runtime.txt[59] file to use it. In your text editor, create this new `runtime.txt` file at the project-level meaning it is in the same directory as `manage.py` and the `Procfile`.

To check the current version of Python run `python --version`.

Shell

```
# Windows
(.venv) > python --version
Python 3.10.2

# macOS
(.venv) % python3 --version
Python 3.10.2
```

In the base directory, right next to the `Procfile`, create a new file called `runtime.txt` and use the following format. Make sure everything is lowercased!

runtime.txt

```
python-3.10.2
```

That's it! Keep in mind we've taken a number of security shortcuts here but the goal is to push our project into production in as few steps as possible. In later chapters we will cover proper security around deployments in depth.

Use `git status` to check our changes, add the new files, and then commit them:

---

[58]https://devcenter.heroku.com/articles/python-support#specifying-a-python-version
[59]https://devcenter.heroku.com/articles/python-runtimes

Shell

```
(.venv) > git status
(.venv) > git add -A
(.venv) > git commit -m "New updates for Heroku deployment"
```

Finally, push to GitHub so we have an online backup of our code changes.

Shell

```
(.venv) > git push -u origin main
```

The last step is to actually deploy with Heroku. If you've ever configured a server yourself in the past, you'll be amazed at how much simpler the process is with a platform-as-a-service provider like Heroku.

Our process will be as follows:

- create a new app on Heroku
- disable the collection of static files (we'll cover this in a later chapter)
- push the code up to Heroku
- start the Heroku server so the app is live
- visit the app on Heroku's provided URL

We can do the first step, creating a new Heroku app, from the command line with `heroku create`. Heroku will create a random name for our app, in my case `fathomless-hamlet-26076`. Your name will be different.

Shell

```
(.venv) > heroku create
Creating app... done, ⬛ fathomless-hamlet-26076
https://fathomless-hamlet-26076.herokuapp.com/ |
https://git.heroku.com/fathomless-hamlet-26076.git
```

The `heroku create` command also creates a dedicated remote named `heroku` for our app. To see this, type `git remote -v`.

Shell

```
> git remote -v
heroku   https://git.heroku.com/fathomless-hamlet-26076.git (fetch)
heroku   https://git.heroku.com/fathomless-hamlet-26076.git (push)
```

This new remote means that as long as we include `heroku` in a command we have the ability to both push and fetch code from Heroku now.

At this point, we only need one set of additional Heroku configurations, which is to tell Heroku to ignore static files like CSS and JavaScript. By default, Django will try to optimize these for us which causes issues. We'll cover this in later chapters so for now just run the following command:

Shell

```
(.venv) > heroku config:set DISABLE_COLLECTSTATIC=1
```

Now we can push our code up to Heroku:

Shell

```
(.venv) > git push heroku main
```

If we had just typed `git push origin main` the code would have been pushed to GitHub, not Heroku. Adding `heroku` to the command sends the code to Heroku. Git itself can be quite confusing initially to understand!

The last step is to make our Heroku app live. As websites grow in traffic they need additional Heroku services but for our basic example we can use the lowest level, `web=1`, which also happens to be free! Type the following command:

Shell

```
(.venv) > heroku ps:scale web=1
```

We're done! The last step is to confirm our app is live and online. If you use the command `heroku open` your web browser will open a new tab with the URL of your app:

Shell

```
(.venv) > heroku open
```

Mine is at `https://fathomless-hamlet-26076.herokuapp.com/`.

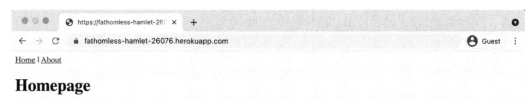

Homepage on Heroku

You do not have to log out or exit from your Heroku app. It will continue running at this free tier on its own, though you should type `deactivate` to leave the local virtual environment and be ready for the next chapter.

Conclusion

Congratulations on building and deploying your second Django project! This time we used templates, class-based views, explored URLs more fully, added basic tests, and used Heroku. If you feel overwhelmed by the deployment process, don't worry. Deployment is hard even with a tool like Heroku. The good news is the steps required are the same for most projects so you can refer to a deployment checklist to guide you each time you launch a new project.

The full source code for this chapter is available on GitHub[60] if you need a reference. In the next chapter we'll move on to our first database-backed project, a *Message Board* website, and see where Django really shines.

---

[60]https://github.com/wsvincent/djangoforbeginners

Chapter 4: Message Board App

In this chapter we will use a database for the first time to build a basic *Message Board* application where users can post and read short messages. We'll explore Django's powerful built-in admin interface which provides a visual way to make changes to our data. And after adding tests we will push our code to GitHub and deploy the app on Heroku.

Thanks to the powerful Django ORM (Object-Relational Mapper), there is built-in support for multiple database backends: PostgreSQL, MySQL, MariaDB, Oracle, and SQLite. This means that we, as developers, can write the same Python code in a `models.py` file and it will automatically be translated into the correct SQL for each database. The only configuration required is to update the DATABASES[61] section of our `django_project/settings.py` file. This is truly an impressive feature!

For local development, Django defaults to using SQLite[62] because it is file-based and therefore far simpler to use than the other database options that require a dedicated server to be running separate from Django itself.

Initial Set Up

Since we've already set up several Django projects at this point in the book, we can quickly run through the standard commands to begin a new one. We need to do the following:

- make a new directory for our code called `message-board`
- install Django in a new virtual environment
- create a new project called `django_project`
- create a new app call `posts`
- update `django_project/settings.py`

In a new command line console, enter the following commands:

---

[61]https://docs.djangoproject.com/en/4.0/ref/databases/
[62]https://www.sqlite.org/

Shell

```
# Windows
> cd onedrive\desktop\code
> mkdir message-board
> cd message-board
> python -m venv .venv
> .venv\Scripts\Activate.ps1
(.venv) > python -m pip install django~=4.0.0
(.venv) > django-admin startproject django_project .
(.venv) > python manage.py startapp posts

# macOS
% cd ~/desktop/code
% mkdir message-board
% cd message-board
% python3 -m venv .venv
% source .venv/bin/activate
(.venv) % python3 -m pip install django~=4.0.0
(.venv) % django-admin startproject django_project .
(.venv) % python3 manage.py startapp posts
```

Next we must alert Django to the new app, posts, by adding it to the top of the INSTALLED_APPS section of our django_project/settings.py file.

Code

```
# django_project/settings.py
INSTALLED_APPS = [
    "django.contrib.admin",
    "django.contrib.auth",
    "django.contrib.contenttypes",
    "django.contrib.sessions",
    "django.contrib.messages",
    "django.contrib.staticfiles",
    "posts.apps.PostsConfig",  # new
]
```

Then execute the migrate command to create an initial database based on Django's default settings.

Shell

```
(.venv) > python manage.py migrate
```

If you look inside our directory with the `ls` command, you'll see the `db.sqlite3` file representing our SQLite database.

Shell

```
(.venv) > ls
.venv       db.sqlite3      django_project      manage.py       posts
```

Technically, a `db.sqlite3` file is created the first time you run *either* `migrate` or `runserver`, however `migrate` will sync the database with the current state of any database models contained in the project and listed in `INSTALLED_APPS`. In other words, to make sure the database reflects the current state of your project you'll need to run `migrate` (and also `makemigrations`) each time you update a model. More on this shortly.

To confirm everything works correctly, spin up our local server.

Shell

```
(.venv) > python manage.py runserver
```

In your web browser, navigate to `http://127.0.0.1:8000/` to see the familiar Django welcome page.

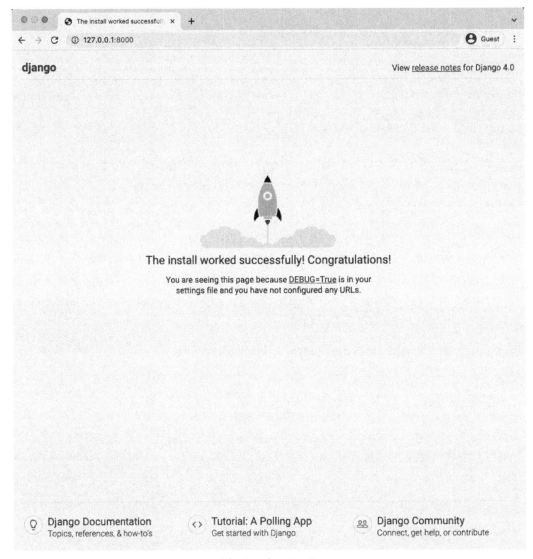

Django welcome page

Create a Database Model

Our first task is to create a database model where we can store and display posts from our users. Django's ORM will automatically turn this model into a database table for us. In a real-world

Django project, there are often many complex, interconnected database models but in our simple message board app we only need one.

Open the `posts/models.py` file and look at the default code which Django provides:

Code

```
# posts/models.py
from django.db import models

# Create your models here
```

Django imports a module, `models`, to help us build new database models which will "model" the characteristics of the data in our database. We want to create a model to store the textual content of a message board post, which we can do as follows:

Code

```
# posts/models.py
from django.db import models


class Post(models.Model):  # new
    text = models.TextField()
```

Note that we've created a new database model called `Post` which has the database field `text`. We've also specified the *type of content* it will hold, `TextField()`. Django provides many model fields[63] supporting common types of content such as characters, dates, integers, emails, and so on.

Activating models

Now that our new model is created we need to activate it. Going forward, whenever we create or modify an existing model we'll need to update Django in a two-step process:

1. First, we create a migrations file with the `makemigrations` command. Migration files create a reference of any changes to the database models which means we can track changes–and debug errors as necessary–over time.

---

[63]https://docs.djangoproject.com/en/4.0/ref/models/fields/

2. Second, we build the actual database with the `migrate` command which executes the instructions in our migrations file.

Make sure the local server is stopped by typing `Control+c` on the command line and then run the commands `python manage.py makemigrations posts` and `python manage.py migrate`.

Shell

```
(.venv) > python manage.py makemigrations posts
Migrations for 'posts':
  posts/migrations/0001_initial.py
    - Create model Post

(.venv) > python manage.py migrate
Operations to perform:
  Apply all migrations: admin, auth, contenttypes, posts, sessions
Running migrations:
  Applying posts.0001_initial... OK
```

Note that you don't *have* to include a name after `makemigrations`. If you simply run `python manage.py makemigrations`, a migrations file will be created for *all* available changes throughout the Django project. That is fine in a small project such as ours with only a single app, but most Django projects have more than one app! Therefore ,if you made model changes in multiple apps the resulting migrations file would include *all* those changes! This is not ideal. Migrations file should be as small and concise as possible as this makes it easier to debug in the future or even roll back changes as needed. Therefore, as a best practice, adopt the habit of always including the name of an app when executing the `makemigrations` command!

Django Admin

One of Django's killer features is its robust admin interface that provides a visual way to interact with data. It came about because Django was originally built[64] as a newspaper CMS (Content Management System). The idea was that journalists could write and edit their stories in the admin without needing to touch "code." Over time, the built-in admin app has evolved into a fantastic, out-of-the-box tool for managing all aspects of a Django project.

---

[64]https://docs.djangoproject.com/en/4.0/faq/general/

To use the Django admin, we first need to create a superuser who can log in. In your command line console, type python manage.py createsuperuser and respond to the prompts for a username, email, and password:

Shell

```
(.venv) > python manage.py createsuperuser
Username (leave blank to use 'wsv'): wsv
Email: will@wsvincent.com
Password:
Password (again):
Superuser created successfully.
```

When you type your password, it will not appear visible in the command line console for security reasons. Restart the Django server with python manage.py runserver and in your web browser go to http://127.0.0.1:8000/admin/. You should see the log in screen for the admin:

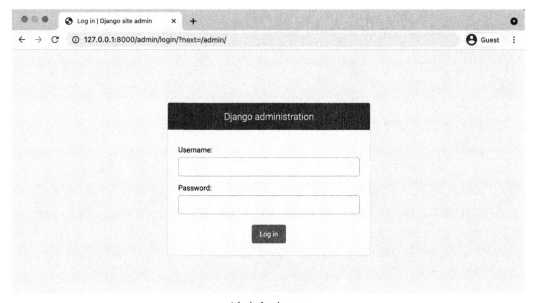

Admin log in page

Log in by entering the username and password you just created. You will see the Django admin homepage next:

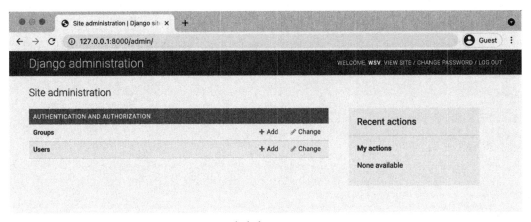

Admin homepage

But where is our posts app? It's not displayed on the main admin page! Just as we must explicitly add new apps to the INSTALLED_APPS config, so, too, must we update an app's admin.py file for it to appear in the admin.

In your text editor open up posts/admin.py and add the following code so that the Post model is displayed.

Code

```
# posts/admin.py
from django.contrib import admin

from .models import Post

admin.site.register(Post)
```

Django now knows that it should display our posts app and its database model Post on the admin page. If you refresh your browser you'll see that it appears:

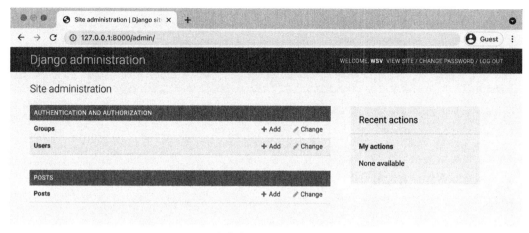

Admin homepage updated

Let's create our first message board post for our database. Click on the + Add button opposite Posts and enter your own content in the Text form field.

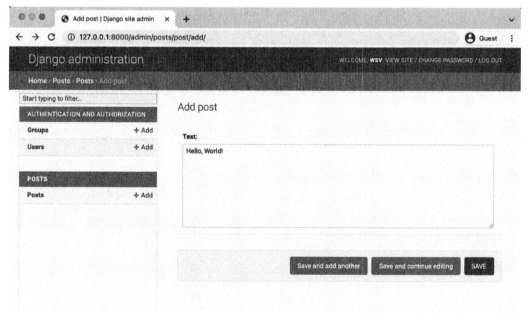

Admin new entry

Then click the "Save" button, which will redirect you to the main Post page. However if you look closely, there's a problem: our new entry is called "Post object (1)" which isn't very descriptive!

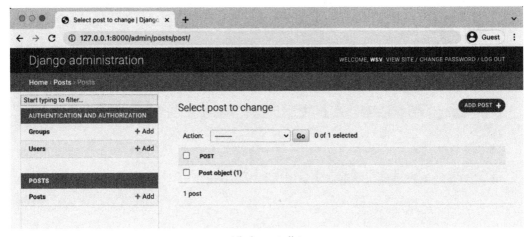

Admin posts list

Let's change that. Within the posts/models.py file, add a new function __str__ as follows:

Code

```
# posts/models.py
from django.db import models


class Post(models.Model):
    text = models.TextField()

    def __str__(self):  # new
        return self.text[:50]
```

This will display the first 50 characters of the text field. If you refresh your Admin page in the browser, you'll see it's changed to a much more descriptive and helpful representation of our database entry.

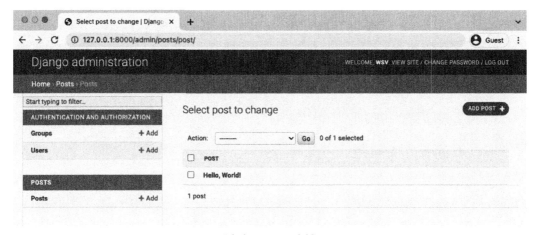

Admin posts readable

Much better! It's a best practice to add `str()` methods to all of your models to improve their readability.

Views/Templates/URLs

In order to display our database content on our homepage, we have to wire up our views, templates, and URLs. This pattern should start to feel familiar now.

Let's begin with the view. Earlier in the book we used the built-in generic TemplateView[65] to display a template file on our homepage. Now we want to list the contents of our database model. Fortunately this is also a common task in web development and Django comes equipped with the generic class-based ListView[66].

In the `posts/views.py` file enter the Python code below:

---

[65]https://docs.djangoproject.com/en/4.0/ref/class-based-views/base/#django.views.generic.base.TemplateView

[66]https://docs.djangoproject.com/en/4.0/ref/class-based-views/generic-display/#listview

Code

```
# posts/views.py
from django.views.generic import ListView
from .models import Post


class HomePageView(ListView):
    model = Post
    template_name = "home.html"
```

On the first line we're importing `ListView` and in the second line we import the `Post` model. In the view, `HomePageView`, we subclass `ListView` and specify the correct model and template.

Our view is complete which means we still need to configure our URLs and make our template. Let's start with the template. Create a new directory called `templates`.

Shell

```
(.venv) > mkdir templates
```

Then update the `DIRS` field in our `django_project/settings.py` file so that Django knows to look in this new templates directory.

Code

```
# django_project/settings.py
TEMPLATES = [
    {
        ...
        "DIRS": [BASE_DIR / "templates"],   # new
        ...
    },
]
```

In your text editor, create a new file called `templates/home.html`. ListView automatically returns to us a context variable called `<model>_list`, where `<model>` is our model name, that we can loop over via the built-in for[67] template tag. We'll create our own variable called `post` and can then access the desired field we want displayed, `text`, as `post.text`.

---

[67]https://docs.djangoproject.com/en/4.0/ref/templates/builtins/#std:templatetag-for

Code

```
<!-- templates/home.html -->
<h1>Message board homepage</h1>
<ul>
  {% for post in post_list %}
    <li>{{ post.text }}</li>
  {% endfor %}
</ul>
```

The last step is to set up our URLs. Let's start with the `django_project/urls.py` file where we include our `posts` app and add `include` on the second line.

Code

```
# django_project/urls.py
from django.contrib import admin
from django.urls import path, include  # new

urlpatterns = [
    path("admin/", admin.site.urls),
    path("", include("posts.urls")),  # new
]
```

Then in your text editor create a new `urls.py` file within the `posts` app and update it like so:

Code

```
# posts/urls.py
from django.urls import path
from .views import HomePageView

urlpatterns = [
    path("", HomePageView.as_view(), name="home"),
]
```

Restart the server with `python manage.py runserver` and navigate to our homepage, which now lists out our message board post.

Homepage with posts

We're basically done at this point, but let's create a few more message board posts in the Django admin to confirm that they will display correctly on the homepage.

Adding New Posts

To add new posts to our message board, go back into the Admin and create two more posts. If you then return to the homepage you'll see it automatically displays the formatted posts. Woohoo!

Everything works so it is a good time to initialize our directory and create a `.gitignore` file. In your text editor create a new `.gitignore` file and add one line:

.gitignore
```
.venv/
```

Then run `git status` again to confirm the `.venv` directory is being ignored, use `git add -A` to add the intended files/directories, and add an initial commit message.

Shell
```
(.venv) > git status
(.venv) > git add -A
(.venv) > git commit -m "initial commit"
```

Shell

```
(.venv) > git init
(.venv) > git add -A
(.venv) > git commit -m "initial commit"
```

Tests

In the previous chapter we were only testing static pages so we used SimpleTestCase[68]. Now that our project works with a database, we need to use TestCase[69], which will let us create a test database we can check against. In other words, we don't need to run tests on our *actual* database but instead can make a separate test database, fill it with sample data, and then test against it which is a much safer and more performant approach.

We will use the hook setUpTestData()[70] to create our test data. This was added to Django 1.8 and is much faster than using the `setUp()` hook from Python's unittest because it creates the test data only once per test case rather than per test. It is still common, however, to see Django projects that rely on `setUp()` instead. Converting any such tests over to `setUpTestData` is a reliable way to speed up a test suite and should be done!

Our `Post` model contains only one field, `text`, so let's set up our data and then check that it is stored correctly in the database. All test methods must start with the phrase `test*` so that Django knows to test them! The code will look like this:

---

[68]https://docs.djangoproject.com/en/4.0/topics/testing/tools/#django.test.SimpleTestCase
[69]https://docs.djangoproject.com/en/4.0/topics/testing/tools/#django.test.TestCase
[70]https://docs.djangoproject.com/en/4.0/topics/testing/tools/#django.test.TestCase.setUpTestData

Code

```
# posts/tests.py
from django.test import TestCase

from .models import Post


class PostTests(TestCase):
    @classmethod
    def setUpTestData(cls):
        cls.post = Post.objects.create(text="This is a test!")

    def test_model_content(self):
        self.assertEqual(self.post.text, "This is a test!")
```

At the top we import TestCase and our Post model. Then we create a test class, PostTests, that extends TestCase and uses the built-in method setUpTestData to create initial data. In this instance, we only have one item stored as cls.post that can then be referred to in any subsequent tests within the class as self.post. Our first test, test_model_content, uses assertEqual to check that the content of the text field matches what we expect.

Go ahead and run the test on the command line with command python manage.py test.

Shell

```
(.venv) > python manage.py test
Creating test database for alias 'default'...
System check identified no issues (0 silenced).
.
----------------------------------------------------------------
Ran 1 test in 0.001s

OK
Destroying test database for alias 'default'...
```

It passed! Why does the output say only one test was run when we have two functions? Again, only functions that start with the name test* will be run! So while we can use set up functions and classes to help with our tests, unless a function is so named it won't be run on its own as a standalone test when we execute the python manage.py test command.

Moving along it is time to check our URLs, views, and templates in a manner similar to the previous chapter. We will want to check the following four things for our message board page:

- URL exists at / and returns a 200 HTTP status code
- URL is available by its name of "home"
- Correct template is used called "home.html"
- Homepage content matches what we expect in the database

We can include all of these tests in our existing `PostTests` class since there is only one webpage in this project. Make sure to import `reverse` at the top of the page and add the four tests as follows:

Code

```
# posts/tests.py
from django.test import TestCase
from django.urls import reverse  # new

from .models import Post


class PostTests(TestCase):
    @classmethod
    def setUpTestData(cls):
        cls.post = Post.objects.create(text="This is a test!")

    def test_model_content(self):
        self.assertEqual(self.post.text, "This is a test!")

    def test_url_exists_at_correct_location(self):  # new
        response = self.client.get("/")
        self.assertEqual(response.status_code, 200)

    def test_url_available_by_name(self):  # new
        response = self.client.get(reverse("home"))
        self.assertEqual(response.status_code, 200)

    def test_template_name_correct(self):  # new
        response = self.client.get(reverse("home"))
        self.assertTemplateUsed(response, "home.html")

    def test_template_content(self):  # new
```

```
        response = self.client.get(reverse("home"))
        self.assertContains(response, "This is a test!")
```

If you run our tests again you should see that they all pass.

Shell

```
(.venv) > python manage.py test
Creating test database for alias 'default'...
System check identified no issues (0 silenced).
.
-------------------------------------------------------------------
Ran 5 tests in 0.009s

OK
Destroying test database for alias 'default'...
```

In the previous chapter we discussed how unit tests work best when they are self-contained and extremely verbose. However there is an argument to be made here that the bottom three tests are really just testing that the homepage works as expected: it uses the correct URL name, the intended template name, and contains expected content. We can combine these three tests into one single unit test, test_homepage.

Code

```
# posts/tests.py
from django.test import TestCase
from django.urls import reverse  # new
from .models import Post


class PostTests(TestCase):
    @classmethod
    def setUpTestData(cls):
        cls.post = Post.objects.create(text="This is a test!")

    def test_model_content(self):
        self.assertEqual(self.post.text, "This is a test!")

    def test_url_exists_at_correct_location(self):
        response = self.client.get("/")
        self.assertEqual(response.status_code, 200)
```

```
def test_homepage(self):  # new
    response = self.client.get(reverse("home"))
    self.assertEqual(response.status_code, 200)
    self.assertTemplateUsed(response, "home.html")
    self.assertContains(response, "This is a test!")
```

Run the tests one last time to confirm that they all pass.

Shell

```
(.venv) > python manage.py test
Creating test database for alias 'default'...
System check identified no issues (0 silenced).
.
----------------------------------------------------------------------
Ran 3 tests in 0.008s

OK
Destroying test database for alias 'default'...
```

Ultimately, we want our test suite to cover as much code functionality as possible while also being easy for us to reason about, both the error messages *and* the testing code itself. In my view, this update is easier to read and understand.

We're done adding code for our testing so it's time to commit the changes to git.

Shell

```
(.venv) > git add -A
(.venv) > git commit -m "added tests"
```

GitHub

We also need to store our code on GitHub. You should already have a GitHub account from previous chapters so go ahead and create a new repo called message-board. Select the "Private" radio button.

On the next page scroll down to where it says "or push an existing repository from the command line." Copy and paste the two commands there into your terminal, which should look like like the below after replacing wsvincent (my username) with your GitHub username:

Shell
```
(.venv) > git remote add origin https://github.com/wsvincent/message-board.git
(.venv) > git push -u origin main
```

Heroku Configuration

You should already have a Heroku account set up and installed from Chapter 3. Our deployment checklist contains the same five steps:

- install Gunicorn
- create a requirements.txt file
- update ALLOWED_HOSTS in django_project/settings.py
- create a Procfile
- create a runtime.txt file

First, install Gunicorn with Pip.

Shell
```
(.venv) > python -m pip install gunicorn==20.1.0
```

Then output the contents of our virtual environment to a requirements.txt file.

Shell
```
(.venv) > python -m pip freeze > requirements.txt
```

Previously, we set ALLOWED_HOSTS to *, meaning accept all hosts, but that was a dangerous shortcut. We can-and should-be more specific. The two local hosts Django runs on are localhost:8000 and 127.0.0.1:8000. We also know, having deployed on Heroku previously, that any Heroku site will end with .herokuapp.com. We can add all three hosts to our ALLOWED_HOSTS configuration.

Code

```
# django_project/settings.py
ALLOWED_HOSTS = [".herokuapp.com", "localhost", "127.0.0.1"]
```

Fourth in your text editor create a new `Procfile` in the base directory, next to the `manage.py` file.

Procfile

```
web: gunicorn django_project.wsgi --log-file -
```

And the fifth and final step is to create a `runtime.txt` file, also in the base directory, that specifies what version of Python to run within Heroku.

runtime.txt

```
python-3.10.2
```

We're all done! Add and commit our new changes to git and then push them up to GitHub.

Shell

```
(.venv) > git status
(.venv) > git add -A
(.venv) > git commit -m "New updates for Heroku deployment"
(.venv) > git push -u origin main
```

Heroku Deployment

Make sure you're logged into your correct Heroku account.

Shell

```
(.venv) > heroku login
```

Then run the `create` command and Heroku will randomly generate an app name.

Shell
```
(.venv) > heroku create
Creating app... done, â¬¢ sleepy-brook-64719
https://sleepy-brook-64719.herokuapp.com/ |
https://git.heroku.com/sleepy-brook-64719.git
```

For now, continue to instruct Heroku to ignore static files. We'll cover them in the next section while deploying our *Blog* app.

Shell
```
(.venv) > heroku config:set DISABLE_COLLECTSTATIC=1
```

Push the code to Heroku and add free scaling so it's actually running online, otherwise the code is just sitting there!

Shell
```
(.venv) > git push heroku main
(.venv) > heroku ps:scale web=1
```

You can open the URL of the new project from the command line by typing `heroku open` which will launch a new browser window. To finish up, deactivate the current virtual environment by typing `deactivate` on the command line.

Conclusion

We've now built, tested, and deployed our first database-driven app. While it's deliberately quite basic, we learned how to create a database model, update it with the admin panel, and then display the contents on a web page. That's the good news. The bad news is that if you check your Heroku site in a few days, it's likely whatever posts you've added will be deleted! This is related to how Heroku handles SQLite, but really it's an indication that we should be using a production database like PostgreSQL for deployments, even if we still want to stick with SQLite locally. This is covered in Chapter 16!

In the next section, we'll learn how to deploy with PostgreSQL and build a *Blog* application so that users can create, edit, and delete posts on their own. No admin access required! We'll also add styling via CSS so the site looks better.

Chapter 5: Blog App

In this chapter we will build a *Blog* application that allows users to create, edit, and delete posts. The homepage will list all blog posts and there will be a dedicated detail page for each individual blog post. We'll also introduce CSS for styling and learn how Django works with static files.

Initial Set Up

As covered in previous chapters, our steps for setting up a new Django project are as follows:

- make a new directory for our code called `blog`
- install Django in a new virtual environment called `.venv`
- create a new Django project called `django_project`
- create a new app `blog`
- perform a migration to set up the database
- update `django_project/settings.py`

Let's implement them now in a new command line terminal.

Shell

```
# Windows
> cd onedrive\desktop\code
> mkdir blog
> cd blog
> python -m venv .venv
> .venv\Scripts\Activate.ps1
(.venv) > python -m pip install django~=4.0.0
(.venv) > django-admin startproject django_project .
(.venv) > python manage.py startapp blog
(.venv) > python manage.py migrate

# macOS
% cd ~/desktop/code
```

```
% mkdir blog
% cd blog
% python3 -m venv .venv
% source .venv/bin/activate
(.venv) % python3 -m pip install django~=4.0.0
(.venv) % django-admin startproject django_project .
(.venv) % python3 manage.py startapp blog
(.venv) % python3 manage.py migrate
```

To ensure Django knows about our new app, open your text editor and add the new app to
INSTALLED_APPS in the django_project/settings.py file:

Code

```
# django_project/settings.py
INSTALLED_APPS = [
    "django.contrib.admin",
    "django.contrib.auth",
    "django.contrib.contenttypes",
    "django.contrib.sessions",
    "django.contrib.messages",
    "django.contrib.staticfiles",
    "blog.apps.BlogConfig",  # new
]
```

Spin up the local server using the runserver command.

Shell

```
(.venv) > python manage.py runserver
```

If you navigate to http://127.0.0.1:8000/ in your web browser you should see the friendly
Django welcome page.

Django welcome page

Ok, initial installation complete! Next we'll create our database model for blog posts.

Database Models

What are the characteristics of a typical blog application? In our case, let's keep things simple and assume each post has a title, author, and body. We can turn this into a database model by opening the `blog/models.py` file and entering the code below:

Code

```
# blog/models.py
from django.db import models
from django.urls import reverse


class Post(models.Model):
    title = models.CharField(max_length=200)
    author = models.ForeignKey(
        "auth.User",
        on_delete=models.CASCADE,
    )
    body = models.TextField()

    def __str__(self):
        return self.title

    def get_absolute_url(self):
        return reverse("post_detail", kwargs={"pk": self.pk})
```

At the top, we're importing the class `models` and the handy utility function reverse[71] that allows us to reference an object by its URL template name. More on this shortly.

Next we create a subclass of `models.Model` called `Post` which provides access to everything within django.db.models.Models[72]. Then we can add additional fields and methods as desired. There are many field types available in Django which can be viewed here[73].

Our model has three fields: `title` which is limited to the length to 200 characters; `body` which uses a TextField to automatically expand as needed to fit the user's text, and an `author`

---

[71]https://docs.djangoproject.com/en/4.0/ref/urlresolvers/#reverse
[72]https://docs.djangoproject.com/en/4.0/topics/db/models/
[73]https://docs.djangoproject.com/en/4.0/topics/db/models/#fields

ForeignKey[74] that allows for a *many-to-one* relationship. This means that a given user can be the author of many different blog posts but not the other way around. The reference is to the built-in User model that Django provides for authentication. For all many-to-one relationships such as a ForeignKey we must also specify an on_delete[75] option.

A __str__ method is added to provide a human-readable version of the model in the admin or Django shell. And we also add a get_absolute_url[76] method, which we haven't seen before, that tells Django how to calculate the canonical URL for our model object. It says to use the URL named post_detail and pass in the pk. More on this later as we build out our blog app.

Now that our new database model is created we need to create a new migration record for it and migrate the change into our database. Stop the server with Control+c. This two-step process can be completed with the commands below:

Shell

```
(.venv) > python manage.py makemigrations blog
(.venv) > python manage.py migrate
```

Our database is configured! What's next?

Admin

We need a way to access our data. Enter the Django admin! First, create a superuser account by typing the command below and following the prompts to set up an email and password. Note that when typing your password, it will not appear on the screen for security reasons.

---

[74]https://docs.djangoproject.com/en/4.0/ref/models/fields/#django.db.models.ForeignKey
[75]https://docs.djangoproject.com/en/4.0/ref/models/fields/#django.db.models.ForeignKey.on_delete
[76]https://docs.djangoproject.com/en/4.0/ref/models/instances/#django.db.models.Model.get_absolute_url

Shell

```
(.venv) > python manage.py createsuperuser
Username (leave blank to use 'wsv'): wsv
Email:
Password:
Password (again):
Superuser created successfully.
```

Now start running the Django server again with the command `python manage.py runserver` and navigate over to the admin at `127.0.0.1:8000/admin/`. Log in with your new superuser account.

Oops! Where's our new `Post` model? We forgot to update `blog/admin.py` so let's do that now.

Code

```python
# blog/admin.py
from django.contrib import admin
from .models import Post

admin.site.register(Post)
```

If you refresh the page you'll see the update.

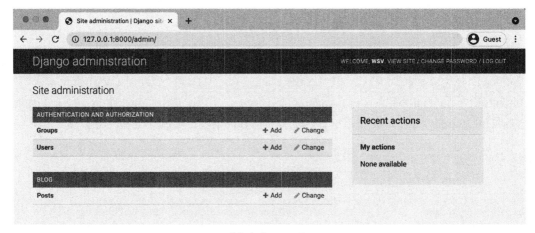

Admin homepage

Let's add two blog posts so we have some sample data to work with. Click on the + `Add` button next to `Posts` to create a new entry. Make sure to add an "author" to each post too since by default all model fields are required.

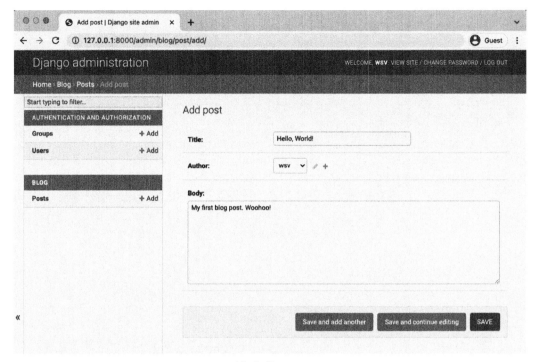

Admin first post

Then create a second post as well.

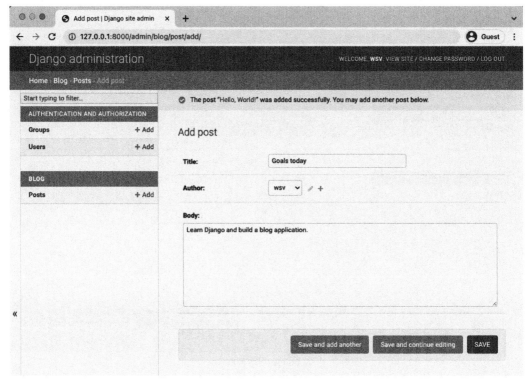

Admin second post

If you try to enter a post without an author you will see an error. If we wanted to change this, we could add field options[77] to our model to make a given field optional or fill it with a default value.

---

[77]https://docs.djangoproject.com/en/4.0/ref/models/fields/#field-options

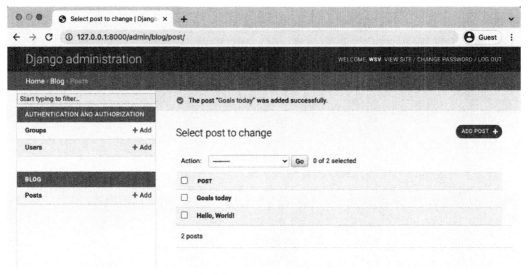

Admin homepage with two posts

Now that our database model is complete we need to create the necessary views, URLs, and templates so we can display the information on our web application.

URLs

We want to display our blog posts on the homepage so, as in previous chapters, we'll first configure our `django_project/urls.py` file and then our app-level `blog/urls.py` file to achieve this.

In your text editor, create a new file called `urls.py` within the `blog` app and update it with the code below.

Code

```
# blog/urls.py
from django.urls import path
from .views import BlogListView

urlpatterns = [
    path("", BlogListView.as_view(), name="home"),
]
```

We're importing our soon-to-be-created views at the top. The empty string, "", tells Python to match all values and we make it a named URL, home, which we can refer to in our views later on. While it's optional to add a named URL[78] it's a best practice you should adopt as it helps keep things organized as your number of URLs grows.

We also should update our django_project/urls.py file so that it knows to forward all requests directly to the blog app.

Code

```
# django_project/urls.py
from django.contrib import admin
from django.urls import path, include   # new

urlpatterns = [
    path("admin/", admin.site.urls),
    path("", include("blog.urls")),   # new
]
```

We've added include on the second line and a URL pattern using an empty string regular expression, "", indicating that URL requests should be redirected as is to blog's URLs for further instructions.

Views

We're going to use class-based views but if you want to see a function-based way to build a blog application, I highly recommend the Django Girls Tutorial[79]. It is excellent.

---

[78]https://docs.djangoproject.com/en/4.0/topics/http/urls/#reverse-resolution-of-urls
[79]https://tutorial.djangogirls.org/en/

In our views file, add the code below to display the contents of our `Post` model using `ListView`.

Code

```
# blog/views.py
from django.views.generic import ListView
from .models import Post


class BlogListView(ListView):
    model = Post
    template_name = "home.html"
```

On the top two lines we import ListView[80] and our database model `Post`. Then we subclass `ListView` and add links to our model and template. This saves us a lot of code versus implementing it all from scratch.

Templates

With our URLs and views now complete, we're only missing the third piece of the puzzle: templates. As we already saw in **Chapter 4**, we can inherit from other templates to keep our code clean. Thus we'll start off with a `base.html` file and a `home.html` file that inherits from it. Then later when we add templates for creating and editing blog posts, they too can inherit from `base.html`.

Start by creating our new `templates` directory.

Shell

```
(.venv) > mkdir templates
```

In your text editor, create two new template files within it called `templates/base.html` and `templates/home.html`.

Then update `django_project/settings.py` so Django knows to look there for our templates.

---

[80]https://docs.djangoproject.com/en/4.0/ref/class-based-views/generic-display/#listview

Code

```
# django_project/settings.py
TEMPLATES = [
    {
        ...
        "DIRS": [BASE_DIR / "templates"],  # new
        ...
    },
]
```

And update the `base.html` template as follows.

Code

```
<!-- templates/base.html -->
<html>
  <head>
    <title>Django blog</title>
  </head>
  <body>
    <header>
      <h1><a href="{% url 'home' %}">Django blog</a></h1>
    </header>
    <div>
      {% block content %}
      {% endblock content %}
    </div>
  </body>
</html>
```

Note that code between `{% block content %}` and `{% endblock content %}` can be filled by other templates. Speaking of which, here is the code for `home.html`.

Code

```html
<!-- templates/home.html -->
{% extends "base.html" %}

{% block content %}
{% for post in post_list %}
  <div class="post-entry">
    <h2><a href="">{{ post.title }}</a></h2>
    <p>{{ post.body }}</p>
  </div>
{% endfor %}
{% endblock content %}
```

At the top, we note that this template extends `base.html` and then wrap our desired code with `content` blocks. We use the Django Templating Language to set up a simple *for loop* for each blog post. Note that `post_list` comes from `ListView` and contains all the objects in our view of the model `post`.

If you start the Django server again with `python manage.py runserver` and refresh the homepage we can see it is working.

Blog homepage with two posts

But it looks terrible. Let's fix that!

Static Files

We need to add some CSS to our project to improve the styling. CSS, JavaScript, and images are a core piece of any modern web application and within the Django world are referred to as "static files." Django provides tremendous flexibility around *how* these files are used, but this can lead to quite a lot of confusion for newcomers.

By default, Django will look within each app for a folder called `static`. In other words, a folder called `blog/static/`. If you recall, this is similar to how `templates` are treated as well.

As Django projects grow in complexity over time and have multiple apps, it is often simpler to reason about static files if they are stored in a single, project-level directory instead. That is the approach we will take here.

Quit the local server with `Control+c` and create a new directory called `static` in the same folder as the `manage.py` file.

Shell

```
(.venv) > mkdir static
```

Then we need to tell Django to look for this new folder when loading static files. If you look at the bottom of the `django_project/settings.py` file, there is already a single line of configuration:

Code

```
# django_project/settings.py
STATIC_URL = "/static/"
```

STATIC_URL[81] is the URL *location* of static files in our project, aka at `/static/`.

By configuring STATICFILES_DIRS[82], we can tell Django where to look for static files beyond just `app/static` folder. In your `django_project/settings.py` file, at the bottom, add the following new line which tells Django to look within our newly-created `static` folder for static files.

---

[81]https://docs.djangoproject.com/en/4.0/ref/settings/#std:setting-STATIC_URL
[82]https://docs.djangoproject.com/en/4.0/ref/settings/#staticfiles-dirs

Code

```
# django_project/settings.py
STATIC_URL = "/static/"
STATICFILES_DIRS = [BASE_DIR / "static"]  # new
```

Next create a `css` directory within `static`.

Shell

```
(.venv) > mkdir static/css
```

In your text editor, create a new file within this directory called `static/css/base.css`.

What should we put in our file? How about changing the title to be red?

Code

```
/* static/css/base.css */
header h1 a {
  color: red;
}
```

Last step now. We need to add the static files to our templates by adding `{% load static %}` to the top of `base.html`. Because our other templates inherit from `base.html`, we only have to add this once. Include a new line at the bottom of the `<head></head>` code that explicitly references our new `base.css` file.

Code

```
<!-- templates/base.html -->
{% load static %}
<html>
  <head>
    <title>Django blog</title>
    <link rel="stylesheet" href="{% static 'css/base.css' %}">
  </head>
  ...
```

Phew! That was a bit of a pain but it's a one-time hassle. Now we can add static files to our `static` directory and they'll automatically appear in all our templates.

Start up the server again with `python manage.py runserver` and look at our updated homepage at `http://127.0.0.1:8000/`.

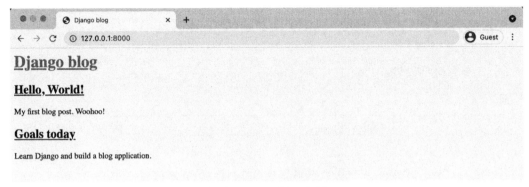

Blog homepage with red title

If you see an error `TemplateSyntaxError` at / that means you forgot to add the `{% load static %}` line at the top. Even after all my years of using Django I still make this mistake all the time! Fortunately, Django's error message says "Invalid block tag on line 4: 'static'. Did you forget to register or load this tag?". This is a pretty accurate description of what happened.

Even with this new styling we can still do a little better. How about if we add a custom font and some more CSS? Since this book is not a tutorial on CSS simply insert the following between `<head></head>` tags to add Source Sans Pro[83], a free font from Google.

Code

```
<!-- templates/base.html -->
{% load static %}
<html>
<head>
  <title>Django blog</title>
  <link href="https://fonts.googleapis.com/css?family=Source+Sans+Pro:400"
    rel="stylesheet">
  <link href="{% static 'css/base.css' %}" rel="stylesheet">
</head>
  ...
```

Then update our css file by copy and pasting the following code:

---

[83]https://fonts.google.com/specimen/Source+Sans+Pro

Code

```css
/* static/css/base.css */
body {
  font-family: 'Source Sans Pro', sans-serif;
  font-size: 18px;
}

header {
  border-bottom: 1px solid #999;
  margin-bottom: 2rem;
  display: flex;
}

header h1 a {
  color: red;
  text-decoration: none;
}

.nav-left {
  margin-right: auto;
}

.nav-right {
  display: flex;
  padding-top: 2rem;
}

.post-entry {
  margin-bottom: 2rem;
}

.post-entry h2 {
  margin: 0.5rem 0;
}

.post-entry h2 a,
.post-entry h2 a:visited {
  color: blue;
  text-decoration: none;
}

.post-entry p {
  margin: 0;
  font-weight: 400;
}
```

```
.post-entry h2 a:hover {
  color: red;
}
```

Refresh the homepage at `http://127.0.0.1:8000/` and you should see the following.

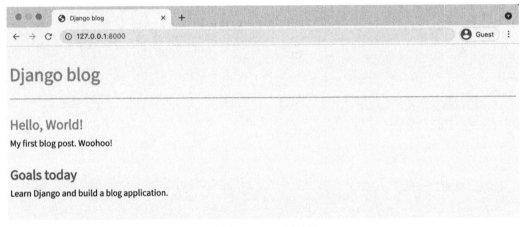

Blog homepage with CSS

Individual Blog Pages

Now we can add the functionality for individual blog pages. How do we do that? We need to create a new view, url, and template. I hope you're noticing a pattern in development with Django now!

Start with the view. We can use the generic class-based DetailView[84] to simplify things. At the top of the file, add `DetailView` to the list of imports and then create a new view called `BlogDetailView`.

---

[84]https://docs.djangoproject.com/en/4.0/ref/class-based-views/generic-display/#django.views.generic.detail.
DetailView

Code

```
# blog/views.py
from django.views.generic import ListView, DetailView  # new
from .models import Post


class BlogListView(ListView):
    model = Post
    template_name = "home.html"


class BlogDetailView(DetailView):  # new
    model = Post
    template_name = "post_detail.html"
```

In this new view, we define the model we're using, Post, and the template we want it associated with, post_detail.html. By default, DetailView will provide a context object we can use in our template called either object or the lowercased name of our model, which would be post. Also, DetailView expects either a primary key or a slug passed to it as the identifier. More on this shortly.

In your text editor create a new template file for a post detail called templates/post_detail.html. Then type in the following code:

Code

```
<!-- templates/post_detail.html -->
{% extends "base.html" %}

{% block content %}
<div class="post-entry">
  <h2>{{ post.title }}</h2>
  <p>{{ post.body }}</p>
</div>
{% endblock content %}
```

At the top we specify that this template inherits from base.html. Then display the title and body from our context object, which DetailView makes accessible as post.

Personally, I found the naming of context objects in generic views extremely confusing when
first learning Django. Because our context object from DetailView is either our model name `post`
or `object` we *could* also update our template as follows and it would work exactly the same.

Code

```
<!-- templates/post_detail.html -->
{% extends "base.html" %}

{% block content %}
<div class="post-entry">
  <h2>{{ object.title }}</h2>
  <p>{{ object.body }}</p>
</div>
{% endblock content %}
```

If you find using `post` or `object` confusing it is possible to explicitly name the context object in
our view using context_object_name[85].

The "magic" naming of the context object is a price you pay for the ease and simplicity of using
generic views, which are great if you know what they're doing but take a little research in the
official documentation to customize.

Ok, what's next? How about adding a new URL path for our view, which we can do as follows.

Code

```
# blog/urls.py
from django.urls import path
from .views import BlogListView, BlogDetailView  # new

urlpatterns = [
    path("post/<int:pk>/", BlogDetailView.as_view(), name="post_detail"),  # new
    path("", BlogListView.as_view(), name="home"),
]
```

All blog post entries will start with `post/`. Next is the primary key for our post entry which will
be represented as an integer, `<int:pk>`. What's the primary key you're probably asking? Django

---

[85]https://docs.djangoproject.com/en/4.0/topics/class-based-views/generic-display/#making-friendly-
template-contexts

automatically adds an auto-incrementing primary key[86] to our database models. So while we only declared the fields `title`, `author`, and `body` on our `Post` model, under-the-hood Django also added another field called `id`, which is our primary key. We can access it as either `id` or `pk`.

The `pk` for our first "Hello, World" post is 1. For the second post, it is 2. And so on. Therefore when we go to the individual entry page for our first post, we can expect that its URL pattern will be `post/1/`.

If you look back to the `get_absolute_url` method on our `Post` model it passes in a `pk` argument because the URL here requires it. Understanding how primary keys and `get_absolute_url` methods work is a very common place of confusion for beginners. It's worth re-reading the previous two paragraphs a few times if it doesn't click. With practice it will become second nature.

If you now start up the server with `python manage.py runserver` you'll see a dedicated page for our first blog post at `http://127.0.0.1:8000/post/1/`.

Blog post one detail

Woohoo! You can also go to `http://127.0.0.1:8000/post/2/` to see the second entry.

To make our life easier, we should update the link on the homepage so we can directly access individual blog posts from there. Swap out the current empty link, `<a href="">`, for `<a href="{% url 'post_detail' post.pk %}">`.

---

[86]https://docs.djangoproject.com/en/4.0/topics/db/models/#automatic-primary-key-fields

Code

```
<!-- templates/home.html -->
{% extends "base.html" %}

{% block content %}
{% for post in post_list %}
<div class="post-entry">
  <h2><a href="{% url 'post_detail' post.pk %}">{{ post.title }}</a></h2>
  <p>{{ post.body }}</p>
</div>
{% endfor %}
{% endblock content %}
```

We start off by using Django's url template tag and specify the URL pattern name of post_detail. If you look at post_detail in our URLs file it expects to be passed an argument pk representing the primary key for the blog post. Fortunately, Django has already created and included this pk field on our post object but we must pass it into the URL by adding it to the template as post.pk.

To confirm everything works, refresh the main page at http://127.0.0.1:8000/ and click on the title of each blog post to confirm the new links work.

Tests

Our *Blog* project has added new functionality we hadn't seen or tested before this chapter. The Post model has multiple fields, we have a user for the first time, and there is both a list view of all blog posts and a detail view for each individual blog post. Quite a lot to test!

To begin we can set up our test data and check the Post model's content. Here's how that might look.

Code

```python
# blog/tests.py
from django.contrib.auth import get_user_model
from django.test import TestCase

from .models import Post


class BlogTests(TestCase):
    @classmethod
    def setUpTestData(cls):
        cls.user = get_user_model().objects.create_user(
            username="testuser", email="test@email.com", password="secret"
        )

        cls.post = Post.objects.create(
            title="A good title",
            body="Nice body content",
            author=cls.user,
        )

    def test_post_model(self):
        self.assertEqual(self.post.title, "A good title")
        self.assertEqual(self.post.body, "Nice body content")
        self.assertEqual(self.post.author.username, "testuser")
        self.assertEqual(str(self.post), "A good title")
        self.assertEqual(self.post.get_absolute_url(), "/post/1/")
```

At the top we imported get_user_model()[87] to refer to our User and then added `TestCase` and the `Post` model. Our class `BlogTests` contains set up data for both a test user and a test post. At the moment, all the tests are focused on the `Post` model so we name our test `test_post_model`. It checks that all three model fields return the expected values. There are also new tests for the `__str__` and `get_absolute_url` methods on our model.

Go ahead and run the tests.

---

[87]https://docs.djangoproject.com/en/4.0/topics/auth/customizing/#django.contrib.auth.get_user_model

Shell

```
(.venv) > python manage.py test
Creating test database for alias 'default'...
System check identified no issues (0 silenced).
.
----------------------------------------------------------------------
Ran 1 test in 0.110s

OK
Destroying test database for alias 'default'...
```

What else to add? We have two types of pages now: a homepage that lists all blog posts and a detail page for each blog post containing its primary key in the URL. In the previous two chapters we implemented tests to check that:

- expected URLs exist and return a 200 status code
- URL names work and return a 200 status code
- correct template name is used
- correct template content is outputted

All four tests need to be included. We *could* have eight new unit tests: four for each of our two page types. Or we could combine them a bit. There isn't really a right or wrong answer here so long as tests are implemented to test functionality and it is clear from their names what went wrong if an error arises.

Here is one way to add these checks to our code:

Code

```
# blog/tests.py
from django.contrib.auth import get_user_model
from django.test import TestCase
from django.urls import reverse  # new

from .models import Post


class BlogTests(TestCase):
    @classmethod
    def setUpTestData(cls):
        cls.user = get_user_model().objects.create_user(
            username="testuser", email="test@email.com", password="secret"
        )

        cls.post = Post.objects.create(
            title="A good title", body="Nice body content", author=cls.user,
        )

    def test_post_model(self):
        self.assertEqual(self.post.title, "A good title")
        self.assertEqual(self.post.body, "Nice body content")
        self.assertEqual(self.post.author.username, "testuser")
        self.assertEqual(str(self.post), "A good title")
        self.assertEqual(self.post.get_absolute_url(), "/post/1/")

    def test_url_exists_at_correct_location_listview(self):  # new
        response = self.client.get("/")
        self.assertEqual(response.status_code, 200)

    def test_url_exists_at_correct_location_detailview(self):  # new
        response = self.client.get("/post/1/")
        self.assertEqual(response.status_code, 200)

    def test_post_listview(self):  # new
        response = self.client.get(reverse("home"))
        self.assertEqual(response.status_code, 200)
        self.assertContains(response, "Nice body content")
        self.assertTemplateUsed(response, "home.html")

    def test_post_detailview(self):  # new
        response = self.client.get(reverse("post_detail",
          kwargs={"pk": self.post.pk}))
        no_response = self.client.get("/post/100000/")
```

```
self.assertEqual(response.status_code, 200)
self.assertEqual(no_response.status_code, 404)
self.assertContains(response, "A good title")
self.assertTemplateUsed(response, "post_detail.html")
```

First we check that URL exists at the proper location for both views. Then we import reverse[88] at the top and create `test_post_listview` to confirm that the named URL is used, returns a 200 status code, contains the expected content, and uses the `home.html` template. For `test_post_-detailview` we have to pass in the `pk` of the our test post to the response. The same template is used but we add new tests for what we *don't want* to see. For example, we don't want a response at the URL `/post/100000/` because we have not created that many posts yet! And we don't want a 404 HTTP status response either. It is always good to sprinkle in examples of incorrect tests that *should* fail to make sure your tests aren't all blindly passing for some reason.

Run the new tests to confirm everything is working.

Shell

```
(.venv) > python manage.py test
Creating test database for alias 'default'...
System check identified no issues (0 silenced).
.....
----------------------------------------------------------------
Ran 5 tests in 0.129s

OK
Destroying test database for alias 'default'...
```

A common gotcha when testing URLs is failing to include the preceding slash `/`. For example, if `test_url_exists_at_correct_location_detailview` checked in the response for `"post/1/"` that would throw a 404 error. However if you check `"/post/1/"` it will be a 200 status response.

Git

Now is also a good time for our first Git commit. First, initialize our directory. Then review all the content we've added by checking the `status`.

---

[88]https://docs.djangoproject.com/en/4.0/ref/urlresolvers/#reverse

Shell

```
(.venv) > git init
(.venv) > git status
```

Oops, there is the .venv directory we do not want to include! In your text editor create a .gitignore file and add one line.

.gitignore

```
.venv/
```

Run git status again to confirm the .venv directory is no longer included. Then add the rest of our work along with a commit message.

Shell

```
(.venv) > git status
(.venv) > git add -A
(.venv) > git commit -m "initial commit"
```

Conclusion

We've now built a basic blog application from scratch! Using the Django admin we can create, edit, or delete the content. And we used DetailView for the first time to create a detailed individual view of each blog post entry.

In the next section, **Chapter 6: Forms**, we'll add forms so we don't have to use the Django admin at all for these changes.

Chapter 6: Forms

In this chapter we'll continue working on our Blog application from **Chapter 5** by adding forms so a user can create, edit, or delete any of their blog entries. HTML forms are one of the more complicated and error-prone aspects of web development because any time you accept user input there are security concerns. All forms must be properly rendered, validated, and saved to the database.

Writing this code by hand would be time-consuming and difficult so Django comes with powerful built-in Forms[89] that abstract away much of the difficulty for us. Django also comes with generic editing views[90] for common tasks like displaying, creating, updating, or deleting a form.

CreateView

To start, update our base template to display a link to a page for entering new blog posts. It will take the form `<a href="{% url 'post_new' %}"></a>` where `post_new` is the name for our URL.

Your updated file should look as follows:

Code

```
<!-- templates/base.html -->
{% load static %}
<html>
  <head>
    <title>Django blog</title>
    <link href="https://fonts.googleapis.com/css?family=\
      Source+Sans+Pro:400" rel="stylesheet">
    <link href="{% static 'css/base.css' %}" rel="stylesheet">
  </head>
  <body>
    <div>
      <header>
```

---

[89]https://docs.djangoproject.com/en/4.0/topics/forms/
[90]https://docs.djangoproject.com/en/4.0/ref/class-based-views/generic-editing/

```
        <div class="nav-left">
          <h1><a href="{% url 'home' %}">Django blog</a></h1>
        </div>
        <div class="nav-right">
          <a href="{% url 'post_new' %}">+ New Blog Post</a>
        </div>
      </header>
      {% block content %}
      {% endblock content %}
    </div>
  </body>
</html>
```

Let's add a new URL for post_new now. Import BlogCreateView (which has not been created yet) at the top and then add a URL path for post/new/. We will give it the URL name of post_new so it can be referred to later in our templates.

Code

```
# blog/urls.py
from django.urls import path
from .views import BlogListView, BlogDetailView, BlogCreateView  # new

urlpatterns = [
    path("post/new/", BlogCreateView.as_view(), name="post_new"),   # new
    path("post/<int:pk>/", BlogDetailView.as_view(), name="post_detail"),
    path("", BlogListView.as_view(), name="home"),
]
```

Simple, right? It's the same url, views, template pattern we've seen before. Now let's create our view by importing a new generic class called CreateView[91] at the top and then subclass it to create a new view called BlogCreateView.

---

[91]https://docs.djangoproject.com/en/4.0/ref/class-based-views/generic-editing/#createview

Code

```
# blog/views.py
from django.views.generic import ListView, DetailView
from django.views.generic.edit import CreateView  # new

from .models import Post


class BlogListView(ListView):
    model = Post
    template_name = "home.html"


class BlogDetailView(DetailView):
    model = Post
    template_name = "post_detail.html"


class BlogCreateView(CreateView):  # new
    model = Post
    template_name = "post_new.html"
    fields = ["title", "author", "body"]
```

Within BlogCreateView we specify our database model, Post, the name of our template, post_-new.html, and explicitly set the database fields we want to expose which are title, author, and body.

The last step is to create our template called post_new.html in the text editor. Then add the following code:

Code

```
<!-- templates/post_new.html -->
{% extends "base.html" %}

{% block content %}
<h1>New post</h1>
<form action="" method="post">{% csrf_token %}
  {{ form.as_p }}
  <input type="submit" value="Save">
</form>
{% endblock content %}
```

Let's breakdown what we've done:

- On the top line we inherit from our base template.
- Use HTML `<form>` tags with the POST method since we're *sending* data. If we were receiving data from a form, for example in a search box, we would use GET.
- Add a `{% csrf_token %}`[92] which Django provides to protect our form from cross-site request forgery. **You should use it for all your Django forms.**
- Then to output our form data we use `{{ form.as_p }}` which renders the specified fields within paragraph `<p>` tags.
- Finally, specify an input type of submit and assign it the value "Save".

To view our work, start the server with `python manage.py runserver` and go to the homepage at `http://127.0.0.1:8000/`.

---

[92]https://docs.djangoproject.com/en/4.0/ref/csrf/

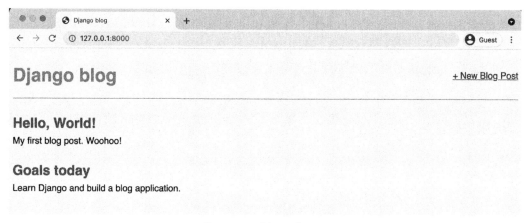

Homepage with new button

Click the "+ New Blog Post" link in the upper righthand corner. It will redirect to web page at http://127.0.0.1:8000/post/new/.

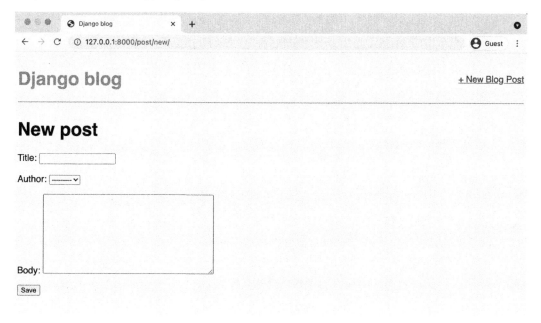

Blog new page

Go ahead and try to create a new blog post and submit it by clicking the "Save" button.

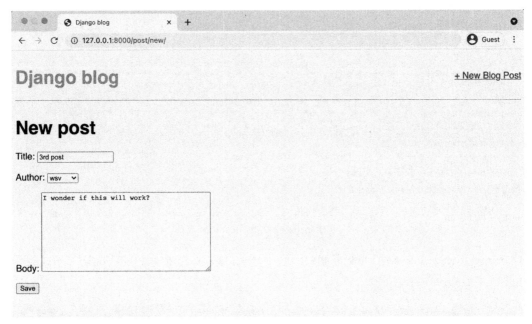

Blog third post save

Upon completion it will redirect to a detail page at `http://127.0.0.1:8000/post/3/` with the post itself. Success!

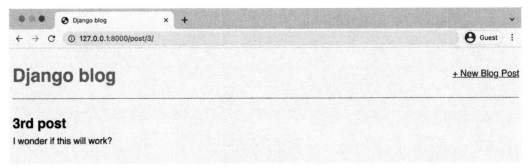

Blog third post page

UpdateView

The process for creating an update form so users can edit blog posts should feel familiar. We'll again use a built-in Django class-based generic view, UpdateView[93], and create the requisite template, url, and view.

To start, let's add a new link to `post_detail.html` so that the option to edit a blog post appears on an individual blog page.

Code

```
<!-- templates/post_detail.html -->
{% extends "base.html" %}

{% block content %}
<div class="post-entry">
  <h2>{{ post.title }}</h2>
  <p>{{ post.body }}</p>
</div>

<a href="{% url 'post_edit' post.pk %}">+ Edit Blog Post</a>
{% endblock content %}
```

We've added a link using `<a href>...</a>` and the Django template engine's `{% url ... %}` tag. Within it, we've specified the target name of our url, which will be called `post_edit` and also passed the parameter needed, which is the primary key of the post `post.pk`.

Next we create the template file for our edit page called `post_edit.html` and add the following code:

---

[93]https://docs.djangoproject.com/en/4.0/ref/class-based-views/generic-editing/#django.views.generic.edit. UpdateView

Code

```
<!-- templates/post_edit.html -->
{% extends "base.html" %}

{% block content %}
<h1>Edit post</h1>
<form action="" method="post">{% csrf_token %}
  {{ form.as_p }}
<input type="submit" value="Update">
</form>
{% endblock content %}
```

We again use HTML `<form></form>` tags, Django's `csrf_token` for security, `form.as_p` to display our form fields with paragraph tags, and finally give it the value "Update" on the submit button.

Now to our view. We need to import `UpdateView` on the second-from-the-top line and then subclass it in our new view `BlogUpdateView`.

Code

```
# blog/views.py
from django.views.generic import ListView, DetailView
from django.views.generic.edit import CreateView, UpdateView  # new

from .models import Post


class BlogListView(ListView):
    model = Post
    template_name = "home.html"


class BlogDetailView(DetailView):
    model = Post
    template_name = "post_detail.html"


class BlogCreateView(CreateView):
    model = Post
    template_name = "post_new.html"
    fields = ["title", "author", "body"]
```

```
class BlogUpdateView(UpdateView):  # new
    model = Post
    template_name = "post_edit.html"
    fields = ["title", "body"]
```

Notice that in `BlogUpdateView` we are explicitly listing the fields we want to use `["title", "body"]` rather than using `"__all__"`. This is because we assume that the author of the post is not changing; we only want the title and text to be editable.

The final step is to update our `urls.py` file as follows. Add the `BlogUpdateView` up top and then the new route at the top of the existing `urlpatterns`.

Code

```
# blog/urls.py
from django.urls import path
from .views import (
    BlogListView,
    BlogDetailView,
    BlogCreateView,
    BlogUpdateView,   # new
)

urlpatterns = [
    path("post/new/", BlogCreateView.as_view(), name="post_new"),
    path("post/<int:pk>/", BlogDetailView.as_view(), name="post_detail"),
    path("post/<int:pk>/edit/", BlogUpdateView.as_view(), name="post_edit"),   # new
    path("", BlogListView.as_view(), name="home"),
]
```

At the top we add our view `BlogUpdateView` to the list of imported views, then created a new url pattern for `/post/pk/edit` and gave it the name `post_edit`.

Now if you click on a blog entry you'll see our new Edit button.

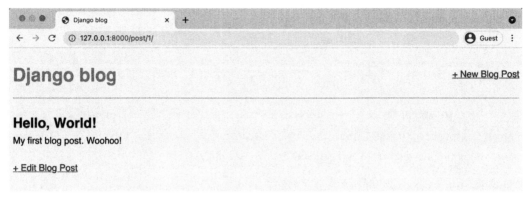

Blog page with edit button

If you click on "+ Edit Blog Post" you'll be redirected to `/post/1/edit/` if it is your first blog post, hence the 1 in the URL. Note that the form is pre-filled with our database's existing data for the post. Let's make a change...

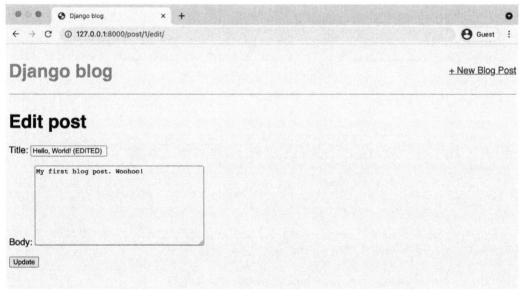

Blog edit page

And after clicking the "Update" button we are redirected to the detail view of the post where you can see the change. This is because of our `get_absolute_url` setting. Navigate to the homepage and you can see the change next to all the other entries.

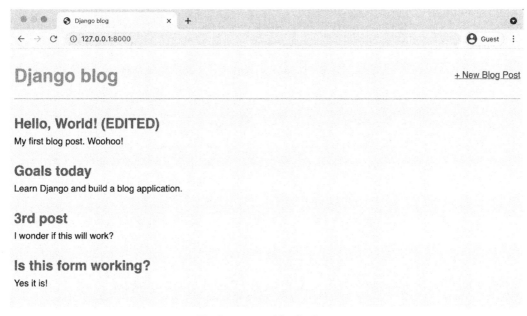

Blog homepage with edited post

DeleteView

The process for creating a form to delete blog posts is very similar to that for updating a post. We'll use yet another generic class-based view, DeleteView[94], create the necessary view, url, and template.

Let's start by adding a link to delete blog posts on our individual blog page, `post_detail.html`.

---

[94]https://docs.djangoproject.com/en/4.0/ref/class-based-views/generic-editing/#deleteview

Code

```
<!-- templates/post_detail.html -->
{% extends "base.html" %}

{% block content %}
<div class="post-entry">
  <h2>{{ post.title }}</h2>
  <p>{{ post.body }}</p>
</div>

<p><a href="{% url 'post_edit' post.pk %}">+ Edit Blog Post</a></p>
<p><a href="{% url 'post_delete' post.pk %}">+ Delete Blog Post</a></p>
{% endblock content %}
```

Then create a new file for our delete page template. It will be called `templates/post_delete.html` and contain the following code:

Code

```
<!-- templates/post_delete.html -->
{% extends "base.html" %}

{% block content %}
<h1>Delete post</h1>
<form action="" method="post">{% csrf_token %}
  <p>Are you sure you want to delete "{{ post.title }}"?</p>
  <input type="submit" value="Confirm">
</form>
{% endblock content %}
```

Note we are using `post.title` here to display the title of our blog post. We could also just use `object.title` as it too is provided by `DetailView`.

Now update the `blog/views.py` file, by importing `DeleteView` and `reverse_lazy` at the top, then create a new view that subclasses `DeleteView`.

Code

```
# blog/views.py
from django.views.generic import ListView, DetailView
from django.views.generic.edit import CreateView, UpdateView, DeleteView  # new
from django.urls import reverse_lazy  # new

from .models import Post


class BlogListView(ListView):
    model = Post
    template_name = "home.html"


class BlogDetailView(DetailView):
    model = Post
    template_name = "post_detail.html"


class BlogCreateView(CreateView):
    model = Post
    template_name = "post_new.html"
    fields = ["title", "author", "body"]


class BlogUpdateView(UpdateView):
    model = Post
    template_name = "post_edit.html"
    fields = ["title", "body"]


class BlogDeleteView(DeleteView):  # new
    model = Post
    template_name = "post_delete.html"
    success_url = reverse_lazy("home")
```

The DeleteView specifies a model which is Post, a template post_delete.html, and a third field called success_url. What does this do? Well, after a blog post is deleted we want to *redirect* the user to another page which is, in our case, the homepage at home.

An astute reader might notice that both CreateView and UpdateView also have redirects yet we did not have to specify a success_url. This is because Django will automatically use get_-

absolute_url() on the model object if it is available. And the only way to know about this trait is to very closely read and remember the docs, where it talks about model forms[95] and success_url. Or more likely to have an error crop up and backtrack to sort out this internal Django behavior.

One final point: we use reverse_lazy[96] here as opposed to just reverse[97] so that it won't execute the URL redirect until our view has finished deleting the blog post.

As a final step, create a URL by importing our view BlogDeleteView and adding a new pattern:

Code

```
# blog/urls.py
from django.urls import path
from .views import (
    BlogListView,
    BlogDetailView,
    BlogCreateView,
    BlogUpdateView,
    BlogDeleteView,  # new
)

urlpatterns = [
    path("post/new/", BlogCreateView.as_view(), name="post_new"),
    path("post/<int:pk>/", BlogDetailView.as_view(), name="post_detail"),
    path("post/<int:pk>/edit/", BlogUpdateView.as_view(),
        name="post_edit"),
    path("post/<int:pk>/delete/", BlogDeleteView.as_view(),
        name="post_delete"),  # new
    path("", BlogListView.as_view(), name="home"),
]
```

If you start the server again with the command python manage.py runserver and refresh any individual post page you'll see our "Delete Blog Post" link.

---

[95]https://docs.djangoproject.com/en/4.0/topics/class-based-views/generic-editing/#model-forms
[96]https://docs.djangoproject.com/en/4.0/ref/urlresolvers/#reverse-lazy
[97]https://docs.djangoproject.com/en/4.0/ref/urlresolvers/#reverse

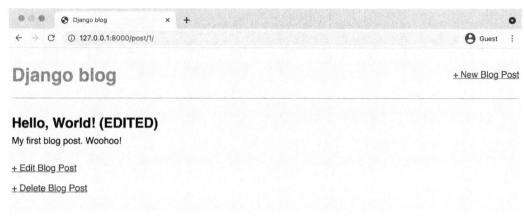

Blog delete post

Clicking on the link takes us to the delete page for the blog post, which displays the name of the blog post.

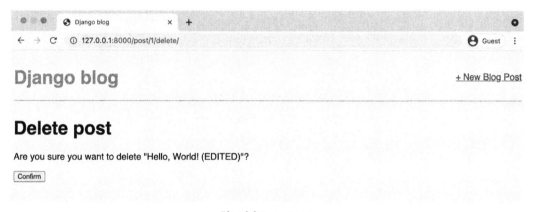

Blog delete post page

If you click on the "Confirm" button, it redirects you to the homepage where the blog post has been deleted!

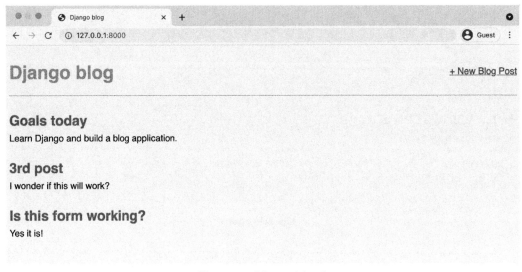

Homepage with post deleted

So it works!

Tests

Time for tests to make sure everything works now–and in the future–as expected. We've added new views for create, update, and delete so that means three new tests:

- `def test_post_createview`
- `def test_post_updateview`
- `def test_post_deleteview`

Update your existing `tests.py` file with new tests below `test_post_detailview` as follows.

Code

```python
# blog/tests.py
    ...
    def test_post_createview(self):  # new
        response = self.client.post(
            reverse("post_new"),
            {
                "title": "New title",
                "body": "New text",
                "author": self.user.id,
            },
        )
        self.assertEqual(response.status_code, 302)
        self.assertEqual(Post.objects.last().title, "New title")
        self.assertEqual(Post.objects.last().body, "New text")

    def test_post_updateview(self):  # new
        response = self.client.post(
            reverse("post_edit", args="1"),
            {
                "title": "Updated title",
                "body": "Updated text",
            },
        )
        self.assertEqual(response.status_code, 302)
        self.assertEqual(Post.objects.last().title, "Updated title")
        self.assertEqual(Post.objects.last().body, "Updated text")

    def test_post_deleteview(self):  # new
        response = self.client.post(reverse("post_delete", args="1"))
        self.assertEqual(response.status_code, 302)
```

For `test_post_createview` we create a new response and check that the page has a 302 redirect status code and the `last()` object created on our model matches the new response. Then `test_post_updateview` sees if we can update the initial post created in `setUpTestData` since that data is available throughout our entire test class. The last new test, `test_post_deleteview`, confirms that a 302 redirect occurs when deleting a post.

There are always more tests that can be added but at least we have some coverage on all our new functionality. Stop the local web server with `Control+c` and run these tests now. They should all pass.

Shell

```
(.venv) > python manage.py test
Creating test database for alias 'default'...
System check identified no issues (0 silenced).
......
----------------------------------------------------------------------
Ran 6 tests in 0.129s

OK
Destroying test database for alias 'default'...
```

Conclusion

With a small amount of code we've built a Blog application that allows for creating, reading, updating, and deleting blog posts. This core functionality is known by the acronym CRUD: *Create-Read-Update-Delete*. While there are multiple ways to achieve this same functionality–we could have used function-based views or written our own class-based views–we've demonstrated how little code it takes in Django to make this happen.

Note, however, a potential security concern: currently *any* user can update or delete blog entries, not just the creator! This is not ideal and indeed Django comes with built-in features to restrict access based on permissions, which we'll cover in-depth in Chapter 14.

But for now our Blog application is working and in the next chapter we'll add user accounts so users can sign up, log in, and log out of the web app.

Chapter 7: User Accounts

So far we've built a working blog application with forms but we're missing a major piece of most web applications: user authentication.

Implementing proper user authentication is famously hard; there are many security gotchas along the way so you really don't want to implement this yourself. Fortunately, Django comes with a powerful, built-in user authentication system[98] that we can use and customize as needed.

Whenever you create a new project, by default Django installs the `auth` app, which provides us with a User object[99] containing:

- username
- password
- email
- first_name
- last_name

We will use this `User` object to implement log in, log out, and sign up in our blog application.

Log In

Django provides us with a default view for a log in page via LoginView[100]. All we need to add are a URL pattern for the auth system, a log in template, and a small update to our `django_project/settings.py` file.

First, update the `django_project/urls.py` file. We'll place our log in and log out pages at the `accounts/` URL. This is a one-line addition on the next-to-last line.

---

[98]https://docs.djangoproject.com/en/4.0/topics/auth/
[99]https://docs.djangoproject.com/en/4.0/ref/contrib/auth/#django.contrib.auth.models.User
[100]https://docs.djangoproject.com/en/4.0/topics/auth/default/#django.contrib.auth.views.LoginView

Code

```
# django_project/urls.py
from django.contrib import admin
from django.urls import path, include

urlpatterns = [
    path("admin/", admin.site.urls),
    path("accounts/", include("django.contrib.auth.urls")),  # new
    path("", include("blog.urls")),
]
```

As the LoginView[101] documentation notes, by default Django will look within a templates directory called `registration` for a file called `login.html` for a log in form. So we need to create a new directory called `registration` and the requisite file within it. From the command line type `Control+c` to quit our local server. Then create the new directory.

Shell

```
(.venv) > mkdir templates/registration
```

And then with your text editor create a new template file, `templates/registration/login.html`, filled with the following code:

Code

```
<!-- templates/registration/login.html -->
{% extends "base.html" %}

{% block content %}
<h2>Log In</h2>
<form method="post">{% csrf_token %}
  {{ form.as_p }}
  <button type="submit">Log In</button>
</form>
{% endblock content %}
```

We're using HTML `<form></form>` tags and specifying the POST method since we're sending data to the server (we'd use GET if we were requesting data, such as in a search engine form). We add

---

[101]https://docs.djangoproject.com/en/4.0/topics/auth/default/#django.contrib.auth.views.LoginView

{% csrf_token %} for security concerns, namely to prevent a CSRF Attack. The form's contents are outputted between paragraph tags thanks to {{ form.as_p }} and then we add a "submit" button.

The final step is we need to specify *where* to redirect the user upon a successful log in. We can set this with the LOGIN_REDIRECT_URL setting. At the bottom of the django_project/settings.py file add the following:

Code

```
# django_project/settings.py
LOGIN_REDIRECT_URL = "home"   # new
```

Now the user will be redirected to the 'home' template which is our homepage. And we're actually done at this point! If you now start up the Django server again with python manage.py runserver and navigate to our log in page at http://127.0.0.1:8000/accounts/login/ you'll see the following:

Log in page

Upon entering the log in info for our superuser account, we are redirected to the homepage. Notice that we didn't add any *view* logic or create a database model because the Django auth system provided both for us automatically. Thanks Django!

Updated Homepage

Let's update our `base.html` template so we display a message to users whether they are logged in or not. We can use the is_authenticated[102] attribute for this.

For now, we can simply place this code in a prominent position. Later on we can style it more appropriately. Update the `base.html` file with new code starting beneath the closing `</header>` tag.

Code

```
<!-- templates/base.html -->
{% load static %}
<html>
  <head>
    <title>Django blog</title>
    <link href="https://fonts.googleapis.com/css?family=Source+Sans+Pro:400"
      rel="stylesheet">
    <link href="{% static 'css/base.css' %}" rel="stylesheet"s>
  </head>
  <body>
    <div>
      <header>
        <div class="nav-left">
          <h1><a href="{% url 'home' %}">Django blog</a></h1>
        </div>
        <div class="nav-right">
          <a href="{% url 'post_new' %}">+ New Blog Post</a>
        </div>
      </header>
      {% if user.is_authenticated %}
        <p>Hi {{ user.username }}!</p>
      {% else %}
        <p>You are not logged in.</p>
        <a href="{% url 'login' %}">Log In</a>
      {% endif %}
    {% block content %}
    {% endblock content %}
    </div>
  </body>
</html>
```

---

[102]https://docs.djangoproject.com/en/4.0/ref/contrib/auth/#django.contrib.auth.models.User.is_
authenticated

If the user is logged in we say hello to them by name; if not we provide a link to our newly created log in page.

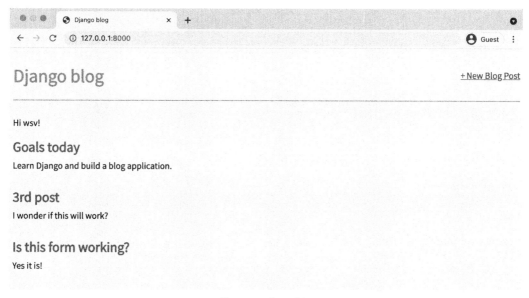

Homepage logged in

It worked! My superuser name is wsv so that's what I see on the page.

Log Out Link

We added template page logic for logged out users but...how do we log out now? We could go into the Admin panel and do it manually, but there's a better way. Let's add a log out link instead that redirects to the homepage. Thanks to the Django auth system, this is dead-simple to achieve.

In our base.html file add a one-line {% url 'logout' %} link for logging out just below our user greeting.

Shell

```
<!-- templates/base.html-->
...
{% if user.is_authenticated %}
  <p>Hi {{ user.username }}!</p>
  <p><a href="{% url 'logout' %}">Log out</a></p>
{% else %}
...
```

That's all we need to do as the necessary view is provided to us by the Django `auth` app. We do need to specify where to redirect a user upon log out though.

Update `django_project/settings.py` to provide a redirect link which is called, appropriately, `LOGOUT_REDIRECT_URL`. We can add it right next to our log in redirect so the bottom of the file should look as follows:

Code

```
# django_project/settings.py
LOGIN_REDIRECT_URL = "home"
LOGOUT_REDIRECT_URL = "home"  # new
```

If you refresh the homepage you'll see it now has a "log out" link for logged in users.

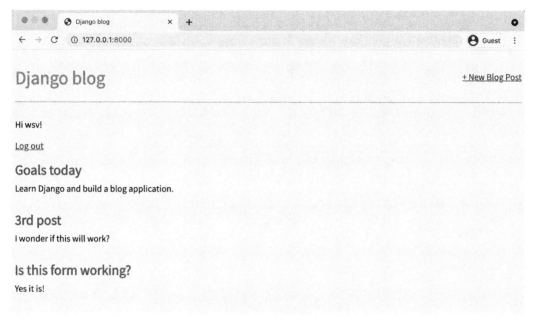

Homepage log out link

And clicking it takes you back to the homepage with a `login` link.

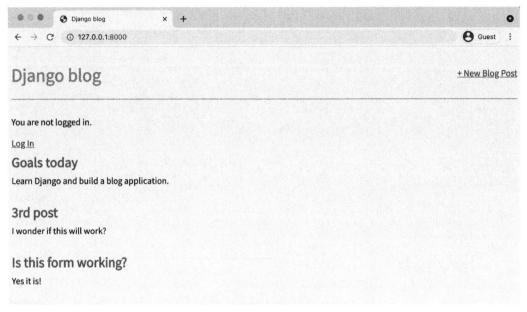

Homepage logged out

Go ahead and try logging in and out several times with your user account.

Sign Up

We need to write our own view for a sign up page to register new users, but Django provides us with a form class, UserCreationForm[103], to make things easier. By default it comes with three fields: `username`, `password1`, and `password2`.

There are many ways to organize your code and URL structure for a robust user authentication system. Stop the local server with `Control+c` and create a dedicated new app, `accounts`, for our sign up page.

---

[103]https://docs.djangoproject.com/en/4.0/topics/auth/default/#django.contrib.auth.forms.UserCreationForm

Shell

```
(.venv) > python manage.py startapp accounts
```

Add the new app to the INSTALLED_APPS setting in our django_project/settings.py file.

Code

```
# django_project/settings.py
INSTALLED_APPS = [
    "django.contrib.admin",
    "django.contrib.auth",
    "django.contrib.contenttypes",
    "django.contrib.sessions",
    "django.contrib.messages",
    "django.contrib.staticfiles",
    "blog.apps.BlogConfig",
    "accounts.apps.AccountsConfig",  # new
]
```

Next add a new URL path in django_project/urls.py pointing to this new app directly **below** where we include the built-in auth app.

Code

```
# django_project/urls.py
from django.contrib import admin
from django.urls import path, include

urlpatterns = [
    path("admin/", admin.site.urls),
    path("accounts/", include("django.contrib.auth.urls")),
    path("accounts/", include("accounts.urls")),  # new
    path("", include("blog.urls")),
]
```

The order of our urls matters here because Django reads this file top-to-bottom. Therefore when we request the /accounts/signup url, Django will first look in auth, not find it, and **then** proceed to the accounts app.

In your text editor, create a file called accounts/urls.py and add the following code:

Code

```
# accounts/urls.py
from django.urls import path
from .views import SignUpView

urlpatterns = [
    path("signup/", SignUpView.as_view(), name="signup"),
]
```

We're using a not-yet-created view called `SignupView` which we already know is class-based since it is capitalized and has the `as_view()` suffix. Its path is just `signup/` so the overall URL path will be `accounts/signup/`.

Now for the view which uses the built-in `UserCreationForm` and generic `CreateView`.

Code

```
# accounts/views.py
from django.contrib.auth.forms import UserCreationForm
from django.urls import reverse_lazy
from django.views.generic import CreateView


class SignUpView(CreateView):
    form_class = UserCreationForm
    success_url = reverse_lazy("login")
    template_name = "registration/signup.html"
```

We're subclassing the generic class-based view `CreateView` in our `SignUpView` class. We specify the use of the built-in `UserCreationForm` and the not-yet-created template at `signup.html`. And we use `reverse_lazy` to redirect the user to the log in page upon successful registration.

Why use `reverse_lazy` here instead of `reverse`? The reason is that for all generic class-based views the URLs are not loaded when the file is imported, so we have to use the lazy form of `reverse` to load them later when they're available.

Now in your text editor create the file `signup.html` within the `templates/registration/` directory. Populate it with the code below.

Code

```
<!-- templates/registration/signup.html -->
{% extends "base.html" %}

{% block content %}
<h2>Sign Up</h2>
<form method="post">{% csrf_token %}
  {{ form.as_p }}
  <button type="submit">Sign Up</button>
</form>
{% endblock content %}
```

This format is very similar to what we've done before. We extend our base template at the top, place our logic between `<form></form>` tags, use the `csrf_token` for security, display the form's content in paragraph tags with `form.as_p`, and include a submit button.

We're now done! To test it out, start up the local server with the command `python manage.py runserver` and navigate to `http://127.0.0.1:8000/accounts/signup/`.

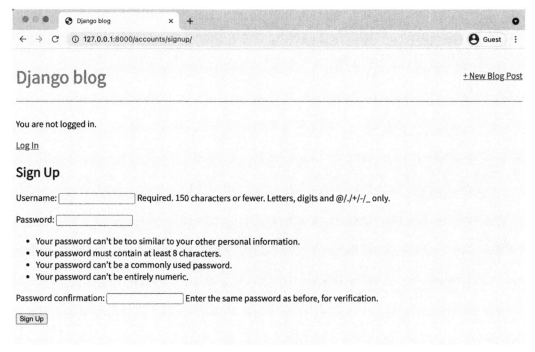

Django sign up page

Notice there is a lot of extra text that Django includes by default. We can customize this using something like the built-in messages framework[104] but for now try out the form.

I've created a new user called "william" and upon submission was redirected to the log in page. Then after logging in successfully with my new user and password, I was redirected to the homepage with our personalized "Hi username" greeting.

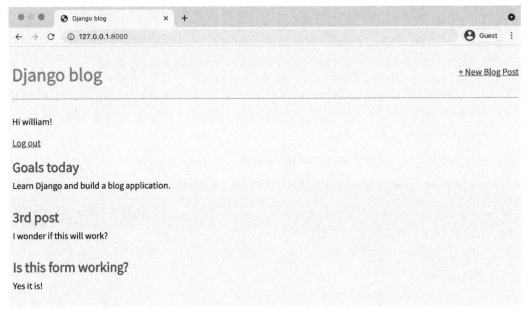

Homepage for user william

Our ultimate flow is therefore: `Signup -> Login -> Homepage`. And of course we can tweak this however we want. The `SignupView` redirects to `login` because we set `success_url = reverse_lazy('login')`. The `Login` page redirects to the homepage because in our `django_-project/settings.py` file we set `LOGIN_REDIRECT_URL = 'home'`.

It can seem overwhelming at first to keep track of all the various parts of a Django project. That's normal. But I promise with time they'll start to make more sense.

---

[104]https://docs.djangoproject.com/en/4.0/ref/contrib/messages/

Sign Up Link

One last improvement we can make is to add a sign up link to the logged out homepage. We can't expect our users to know the correct URL after all! How do we do this? Well, we need to figure out the URL name and then we can pop it into our template. In `accounts/urls.py` we provided it the name of `signup` so that's all we need to add to our `base.html` template with the url template tag[105] just as we've done for our other links.

Add the link for "Sign Up" just below the existing link for "Log In" as follows:

Shell

```
<!-- templates/base.html-->
...
<p>You are not logged in.</p>
<a href="{% url 'login' %}">Log In</a> |
<a href="{% url 'signup' %}">Sign Up</a>
...
```

If you refresh the logged out homepage the sign up link is now visible. Much better!

---

[105]https://docs.djangoproject.com/en/4.0/ref/templates/builtins/#url

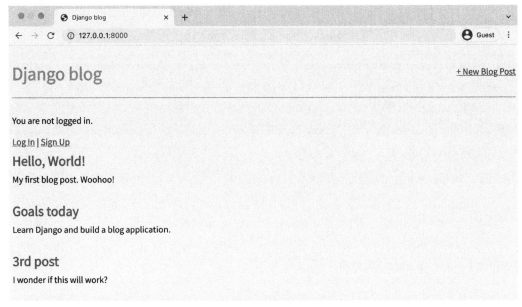

Sign up link

GitHub

It's been a while since we made a `git` commit. Let's do that and then push a copy of our code onto GitHub. First check all the new work that we've done with `git status`.

Shell
```
(.venv) > git status
```

Then add the new content and enter a commit message.

Shell
```
(.venv) > git add -A
(.venv) > git commit -m "forms and user accounts"
```

Create a new repo[106] on GitHub which you can call anything you like. I'll choose the name `blog`. Therefore, *after creating the new repo on the GitHub site*, I can type the following two commands. Make sure to replace my username `wsvincent` with your own from GitHub.

---

[106]https://github.com/new

Shell

```
(.venv) > git remote add origin https://github.com/wsvincent/blog.git
(.venv) > git push -u origin main
```

All done!

Static Files

Previously, we configured our static files by creating a dedicated `static` folder, pointing `STATICFILES_DIRS` to it in our `django_project/settings.py` file, and adding `{% load static %}` to our `base.html` template. But since Django won't serve static files in production, we need a few extra steps now.

The first change is to use Django's `collectstatic` command which compiles all static files throughout the project into a singe directory suitable for deployment. Second, we must set the STATIC_ROOT[107] configuration, which is the *absolute location* of these collected files, to a folder called `staticfiles`. And third, we need to set STATICFILES_STORAGE[108], which is the *file storage engine* used by `collectstatic`.

Here is what the updated `django_project/settings.py` file should look like:

Code

```
# django_project/settings.py
STATIC_URL = "/static/"
STATICFILES_DIRS = [BASE_DIR / "static"]
STATIC_ROOT = BASE_DIR / "staticfiles"    # new
STATICFILES_STORAGE =
    "django.contrib.staticfiles.storage.StaticFilesStorage"  # new
```

For formatting purposes the last line is split in two but it should be one single line in your text editor. Now run the command `python manage.py collectstatic`:

---

[107]https://docs.djangoproject.com/en/4.0/ref/settings/#static-root
[108]https://docs.djangoproject.com/en/4.0/ref/settings/#staticfiles-storage

Shell

```
(.venv) > python manage.py collectstatic
129 static files copied to '/Users/wsv/Desktop/ch7-blog-app-with-users/staticfiles'
```

If you look at your project folder now you'll see there's a new `staticfiles` folder that contains `admin` and `css` folders. The `admin` is the built-in admin's static files, while the `css` is the one we created. Before each new deployment, the `collectstatic` command *must be run* to compile them into this `staticfiles` folder used in production. Since this is an easy step to forget it is often automated in larger projects though doing so is beyond the scope of our current project.

While there are multiple ways to serve these compiled static files in production, the most common approach–and the one we will use here–is to introduce the WhiteNoise[109] package.

To start, install the latest version using `pip`:

Shell

```
(.venv) > python -m pip install whitenoise==5.3.0
```

Then in `django_project/settings.py` there are three updates to make:

- add `whitenoise` to the `INSTALLED_APPS` **above** the built-in `staticfiles` app
- under `MIDDLEWARE` add a new line for `WhiteNoiseMiddleware`
- change `STATICFILES_STORAGE` to use `WhiteNoise`

The updated file should look as follows:

---

[109]http://whitenoise.evans.io/en/stable/

Code

```
# django_project/settings.py
INSTALLED_APPS = [
    "django.contrib.admin",
    "django.contrib.auth",
    "django.contrib.contenttypes",
    "django.contrib.sessions",
    "django.contrib.messages",
    "whitenoise.runserver_nostatic",  # new
    "django.contrib.staticfiles",
    "blog.apps.BlogConfig",
    "accounts.apps.AccountsConfig",
]

MIDDLEWARE = [
    "django.middleware.security.SecurityMiddleware",
    "django.contrib.sessions.middleware.SessionMiddleware",
    "whitenoise.middleware.WhiteNoiseMiddleware",  # new
    "django.middleware.common.CommonMiddleware",
    ...
]

STATIC_URL = "/static/"
STATICFILES_DIRS = [BASE_DIR / "static"]
STATIC_ROOT = BASE_DIR / "staticfiles"
STATICFILES_STORAGE =
    "whitenoise.storage.CompressedManifestStaticFilesStorage"  # new
```

The `STATICFILES_STORAGE` config should also be one line in your text editor. And since the method has changed run `collectstatic` one more time to use `whitenoise` instead:

Shell

```
(.venv) > python manage.py collectstatic
```

There will be a short warning, `This will overwrite existing files! Are you sure you want to do this?` Type "yes" and hit `Enter`. The collected static files are now regenerated in the same `staticfiles` folder using WhiteNoise.

Static files are quite confusing to newcomers, so as a brief recap here are the steps we've executed so far in our *Blog* site. First, for local development back in **Chapter 5**, we created a top-level static folder and updated STATICFILES_DIRS to point to it. In this chapter, we added configurations for STATIC_ROOT and STATICFILES_STORAGE before running collectstatic for the first time, which compiled *all* our static files across the entire project into a single staticfiles folder. Finally, we installed whitenoise, updated INSTALLED_APPS, MIDDLEWARE, and STATICFILES_STORAGE, and re-ran collectstatic.

Most developers, myself included, have trouble remembering all these steps properly and rely on notes as a friendly reminder!

Heroku Config

Now we come for the third time to deploying a website with Heroku. Our deployment checklist is as follows:

- install Gunicorn
- create a requirements.txt file
- update ALLOWED_HOSTS in django_project/settings.py
- create a Procfile
- create a runtime.txt file

Ready? Let's begin. Install Gunicorn as the production web server:

Shell

```
(.venv) > python -m pip install gunicorn==20.1.0
```

Output the contents of the current virtual environment to a requirements.txt file.

Shell

```
(.venv) > python -m pip freeze > requirements.txt
```

Update the existing ALLOWED_HOSTS in django_project/settings.py.

Code

```
# django_project/settings.py
ALLOWED_HOSTS = [".herokuapp.com", "localhost", "127.0.0.1"]  # new
```

And with your text editor create both a new `Procfile` and `runtime.txt` file in the base directory next to the `manage.py` file.

Procfile

```
web: gunicorn django_project.wsgi --log-file -
```

runtime.txt

```
python-3.10.2
```

All set. We can commit our changes and push them up to GitHub.

Shell

```
(.venv) > git status
(.venv) > git add -A
(.venv) > git commit -m "Heroku config"
(.venv) > git push -u origin main
```

Heroku Deployment

To deploy on Heroku first confirm that you're logged in to your existing Heroku account.

Shell

```
(.venv) > heroku login
```

Then run the `create` command which tells Heroku to make a new container for our app to live in. If you just run `heroku create` then Heroku will assign you a random name, however you can specify a custom name but it must be *unique on Heroku*. In other words, since I'm picking the name `dfb-blog` you can't. You need some other combination of letters and numbers.

Shell

```
(.venv) > heroku create dfb-blog
```

Heroku runs Django's `collectstatic` command automatically, which is why in the previous apps, where we had not configured static files, we told Heroku to disable this step with `heroku config:set DISABLE_COLLECTSTATIC=1`. But since we *have* configured static files we'll happily let this happen now as part of the deployment process.

The final step is to push our code to Heroku and add a web process so the dyno is running.

Shell

```
(.venv) > git push heroku main
(.venv) > heroku ps:scale web=1
```

The URL of your new app will be in the command line output or you can run `heroku open` to find it.

SQLite vs PostgreSQL

So far in this book we have been using the file-based SQLite database preconfigured by Django both locally and in deployment. It is much easier to configure and use than a server-based database. However, this convenience comes at a cost. Notably Heroku has an *ephemeral file system* so any changes to the `db.sqlite3` file *in the cloud* will be forgotten whenever a new deployment or server restart occurs. On the free tier we are using, server restarts can happen as often as every 24 hours.

That means that if you make changes to the database locally and push them to production, they will remain. However, if you make updates to the live website such as new blog entries or edits, they will not exist for very long. We need a standalone database engine to persist our data in the cloud which we'll cover in our next project.

Conclusion

With a minimal amount of code, we have added log in, log out, and sign up to our *Blog* website. Under-the-hood Django has taken care of the many security gotchas that can crop up if you try to create your own user authentication flow from scratch. We properly configured static files for production and deployed our website to Heroku. Good job!

In the next chapter, we'll embark on the final major project of the book, a *Newspaper* site which uses a custom user model, advanced user registration flow, enhanced styling via Bootstrap, and email configuration. It also includes proper permissions and authorizations, environment variables, uses PostgreSQL as the production database, and more security improvements to our deployment process.

Chapter 8: Custom User Model

Django's built-in User model[110] allows us to start working with users right away, as we just did with our *Blog app* in the previous chapters. However, the official Django documentation[111] *highly recommends* using a custom user model for new projects. The reason is that if you want to make any changes to the User model down the road--for example adding an `age` field--using a custom user model from the beginning makes this quite easy. But if you do not create a custom user model, updating the default User model in an existing Django project is very, very challenging.

So **always use a custom user model** for all new Django projects. But the approach demonstrated in the official documentation example[112] is actually not what many Django experts recommend. It uses the quite complex `AbstractBaseUser` when if we just use `AbstractUser` instead things are far simpler and still customizable.

Thus we will use `AbstractUser` in this chapter where we start a new *Newspaper* app properly with environment variables and a custom user model. The choice of a newspaper app pays homage to Django's roots as a web framework built for editors and journalists at the Lawrence Journal-World.

Initial Set Up

The first step is to create a new Django project from the command line. We need to do our familiar steps of creating a new directory called `news`, install and activate a new virtual environment called `.venv`, install Django, make a new Django project called `django_project` and then a new app called `accounts`.

Here are the commands to run:

---

[110] https://docs.djangoproject.com/en/4.0/ref/contrib/auth/#django.contrib.auth.models.User
[111] https://docs.djangoproject.com/en/4.0/topics/auth/customizing/#using-a-custom-user-model-when-starting-a-project
[112] https://docs.djangoproject.com/en/4.0/topics/auth/customizing/#a-full-example

Shell

```
# Windows
> cd onedrive\desktop\code
> mkdir news
> cd news
> python -m venv .venv
> .venv\Scripts\Activate.ps1
(.venv) > python -m pip install django~=4.0.0
(.venv) > django-admin startproject django_project .
(.venv) > python manage.py startapp accounts

# macOS
% cd ~/desktop/code
% mkdir news
% cd news
% python3 -m venv .venv
% source .venv/bin/activate
(.venv) % python3 -m pip install django~=4.0.0
(.venv) % django-admin startproject django_project .
(.venv) % python3 manage.py startapp accounts
```

Note that we **did not** run `migrate` to configure our database. It's important to wait until **after** we've created our new custom user model before doing so given how tightly connected the user model is to the rest of Django.

If you navigate to `http://127.0.0.1:8000` in your web browser you'll see the familiar Django welcome screen.

Custom User Model

Creating our custom user model requires four steps:

- update `django_project/settings.py`
- create a new `CustomUser` model
- create new forms for `UserCreationForm` and `UserChangeForm`
- update `accounts/admin.py`

In django_project/settings.py we'll add the accounts app to our INSTALLED_APPS. Then at the bottom of the file use the AUTH_USER_MODEL config to tell Django to use our new custom user model in place of the built-in User model. We'll call our custom user model CustomUser. Since it exists within our accounts app we should refer to it as accounts.CustomUser.

Code

```
# django_project/settings.py
INSTALLED_APPS = [
    "django.contrib.admin",
    "django.contrib.auth",
    "django.contrib.contenttypes",
    "django.contrib.sessions",
    "django.contrib.messages",
    "django.contrib.staticfiles",
    "accounts.apps.AccountsConfig",   # new
]
...
AUTH_USER_MODEL = "accounts.CustomUser"   # new
```

Now update accounts/models.py with a new User model called CustomUser that extends the existing AbstractUser. We also include our a custom field for age here.

Code

```
# accounts/models.py
from django.contrib.auth.models import AbstractUser
from django.db import models


class CustomUser(AbstractUser):
    age = models.PositiveIntegerField(null=True, blank=True)
```

If you read the official documentation on custom user models[113] it recommends using AbstractBaseUser not AbstractUser. This needlessly complicates things in my opinion, especially for beginners.

AbstractBaseUser requires a very fine level of control and customization. We essentially rewrite Django. This *can be* helpful, but if we just want a custom user model that can be updated with additional fields, the better choice is AbstractUser which subclasses AbstractBaseUser. In other

---

[113]https://docs.djangoproject.com/en/4.0/topics/auth/customizing/#specifying-a-custom-user-model

words, we write much less code and have less opportunity to mess things up. It's the better choice unless you really know what you're doing with Django!

Note that we use both null[114] and blank[115] with our age field. These two terms are easy to confuse but quite distinct:

- null is **database-related**. When a field has null=True it can store a database entry as NULL, meaning no value.
- blank is **validation-related**. If blank=True then a form will allow an empty value, whereas if blank=False then a value is required.

In practice, null and blank are commonly used together in this fashion so that a form allows an empty value and the database stores that value as NULL.

A common gotcha to be aware of is that the **field type** dictates how to use these values. Whenever you have a string-based field like CharField or TextField, setting both null and blank as we've done will result in two possible values for "no data" in the database. Which is a bad idea. The Django convention is instead to use the empty string "", not NULL.

Forms

If we step back for a moment, what are the two ways in which we would interact with our new CustomUser model? One case is when a user signs up for a new account on our website. The other is within the admin app which allows us, as superusers, to modify existing users. So we'll need to update the two built-in forms for this functionality: UserCreationForm[116] and UserChangeForm[117].

Create a new file called accounts/forms.py and update it with the following code to extend the existing UserCreationForm and UserChangeForm forms.

---

[114]https://docs.djangoproject.com/en/4.0/ref/models/fields/#null
[115]https://docs.djangoproject.com/en/4.0/ref/models/fields/#blank
[116]https://docs.djangoproject.com/en/4.0/topics/auth/default/#django.contrib.auth.forms.UserCreationForm
[117]https://docs.djangoproject.com/en/4.0/topics/auth/default/#django.contrib.auth.forms.UserChangeForm

Code

```
# accounts/forms.py
from django.contrib.auth.forms import UserCreationForm, UserChangeForm

from .models import CustomUser


class CustomUserCreationForm(UserCreationForm):
    class Meta(UserCreationForm):
        model = CustomUser
        fields = UserCreationForm.Meta.fields + ("age",)


class CustomUserChangeForm(UserChangeForm):
    class Meta:
        model = CustomUser
        fields = UserChangeForm.Meta.fields
```

For both new forms we are using the Meta class[118] to override the default fields by setting the model to our CustomUser and using the default fields via Meta.fields which includes *all* default fields. To add our custom age field we simply tack it on at the end and it will display automatically on our future sign up page. Pretty slick, no?

The concept of fields on a form can be confusing at first so let's take a moment to explore it further. Our CustomUser model contains all the fields of the default User model **and** our additional age field which we set.

But what are these default fields? It turns out there are many[119] including username, first_name, last_name, email, password, groups, and more. Yet when a user signs up for a new account on Django the default form only asks for a username, email, and password. This tells us that the default setting for fields on UserCreationForm is just username, email, and password even though there are many more fields available.

This might not click for you since understanding forms and models properly takes some time. In the next chapter we will create our own sign up, log in, and log out pages which will tie together our CustomUser model and forms more clearly. So hang tight!

---

[118] https://docs.djangoproject.com/en/4.0/topics/forms/modelforms/#overriding-the-default-fields
[119] https://docs.djangoproject.com/en/4.0/ref/contrib/auth/#django.contrib.auth.models.User

The final step we need is to update our admin.py file since Admin is tightly coupled to the default User model. We will extend the existing UserAdmin[120] class to use our new CustomUser model. To control which fields are listed we use list_display[121]. But to actually edit and add new custom fields, like age, we must also add fieldsets[122] (for fields used in editing users) and add_fieldsets (for fields used when creating a user).

Here is what the complete code looks like:

Code

```
# accounts/admin.py
from django.contrib import admin
from django.contrib.auth.admin import UserAdmin

from .forms import CustomUserCreationForm, CustomUserChangeForm
from .models import CustomUser


class CustomUserAdmin(UserAdmin):
    add_form = CustomUserCreationForm
    form = CustomUserChangeForm
    model = CustomUser
    list_display = [
        "email",
        "username",
        "age",
        "is_staff",
    ]
    fieldsets = UserAdmin.fieldsets + ((None, {"fields": ("age",)}),)
    add_fieldsets = UserAdmin.add_fieldsets + ((None, {"fields": ("age",)}),)


admin.site.register(CustomUser, CustomUserAdmin)
```

Ok we're done! Type Control+c to stop the local server and go ahead and run makemigrations and migrate for the first time to create a new database that uses the custom user model.

---

[120] https://docs.djangoproject.com/en/4.0/topics/auth/customizing/#extending-the-existing-user-model
[121] https://docs.djangoproject.com/en/4.0/ref/contrib/admin/#django.contrib.admin.ModelAdmin.list_display
[122] https://docs.djangoproject.com/en/4.0/topics/auth/customizing/#custom-users-and-django-contrib-admin

Shell

```
(.venv) > python manage.py makemigrations accounts
Migrations for 'accounts':
  accounts/migrations/0001_initial.py
    - Create model CustomUser

(.venv) > python manage.py migrate
Operations to perform:
  Apply all migrations: accounts, admin, auth, contenttypes, sessions
Running migrations:
  Applying contenttypes.0001_initial... OK
  Applying contenttypes.0002_remove_content_type_name... OK
  Applying auth.0001_initial... OK
  Applying auth.0002_alter_permission_name_max_length... OK
  Applying auth.0003_alter_user_email_max_length... OK
  Applying auth.0004_alter_user_username_opts... OK
  Applying auth.0005_alter_user_last_login_null... OK
  Applying auth.0006_require_contenttypes_0002... OK
  Applying auth.0007_alter_validators_add_error_messages... OK
  Applying auth.0008_alter_user_username_max_length... OK
  Applying auth.0009_alter_user_last_name_max_length... OK
  Applying auth.0010_alter_group_name_max_length... OK
  Applying auth.0011_update_proxy_permissions... OK
  Applying auth.0012_alter_user_first_name_max_length... OK
  Applying accounts.0001_initial... OK
  Applying admin.0001_initial... OK
  Applying admin.0002_logentry_remove_auto_add... OK
  Applying admin.0003_logentry_add_action_flag_choices... OK
  Applying sessions.0001_initial... OK
```

Superuser

Let's create a superuser account to confirm that everything is working as expected. On the command line type the following command and go through the prompts.

Shell

```
(.venv) > python manage.py createsuperuser
```

Make sure your superuser email account is one that actually works. We will use it later on to verify email integration. But the fact that this flow here works is the first proof our custom user model works is set up correctly. Let's view things in the admin too to be extra sure.

Start up the web server.

Shell

```
(.venv) > python manage.py runserver
```

Then navigate to the admin at `http://127.0.0.1:8000/admin` and log in. If you click on the link for "Users" you should see your superuser account as well as the default fields of Email Address, Username, Age, and Staff Status. These were set in `list_display` in our `admin.py` file.

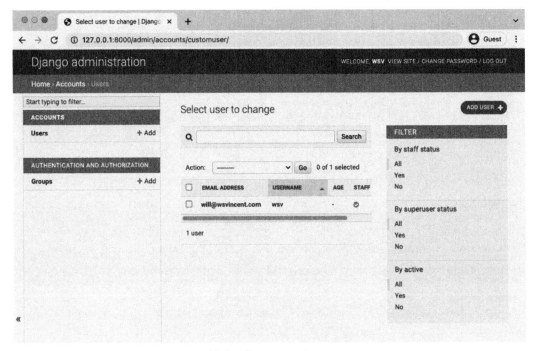

Admin select user to change

The `age` field is empty because we have yet to set it yet. The default prompt for creating a superuser does not ask for it however in the next chapter we will see it is automatically included in our sign up form.

If you do wish to set the age now that is possible because we set the `fieldsets` section. Click on the highlighted link for your superuser's email address which brings up the edit user interface.

Refresh the page and you should see the update. If you scroll to the bottom there is the `age` field we added. Go ahead and enter your age. Then click on "Save".

Admin edit age

It will automatically redirect back to the main Users page listing our superuser. Note that the age field is now updated.

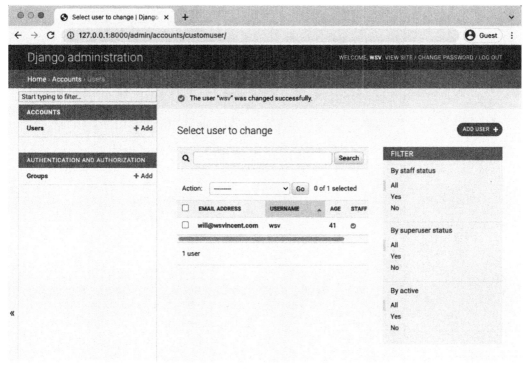

Admin updated age

Conclusion

With our custom user model complete, we can now focus on building out the rest of our *Newspaper* website. In the next chapter we will configure and customize sign up, log in, and log out pages.

Chapter 9: User Authentication

Now that we have a working custom user model we can add the functionality every website needs: the ability to sign up, log in, and log out users. Django provides everything we need for log in and log out but we will need to create our own form to sign up new users. We'll also build a basic homepage with links to all three features so we don't have to type in the URLs by hand every time.

Templates

By default, the Django template loader looks for templates in a nested structure within each app. The structure `accounts/templates/accounts/home.html` would be needed for a `home.html` template within the `accounts` app. But a single `templates` directory within `django_project` approach is cleaner and scales better so that's what we'll use.

Let's create a new `templates` directory and within it a `registration` directory as that's where Django will look for templates related to log in and sign up.

Shell

```
(.venv) > mkdir templates
(.venv) > mkdir templates/registration
```

Now we need to tell Django about this new directory by updating the configuration for `"DIRS"` in `django_project/settings.py`. This is a one-line change.

Code

```
# django_project/settings.py
TEMPLATES = [
    {
        ...
        "DIRS": [BASE_DIR / "templates"],  # new
        ...
    }
]
```

If you think about what happens when you log in or log out of a site, you are immediately redirected to a subsequent page. We need to tell Django where to send users in each case. The LOGIN_REDIRECT_URL and LOGOUT_REDIRECT_URL settings do that. We'll configure both to redirect to our homepage which will have the named URL of 'home'.

Remember that when we create our URL routes we have the option to add a name to each one. So when we make the homepage URL we'll make sure to call it 'home'.

Add these two lines at the bottom of the django_project/settings.py file.

Code

```
# django_project/settings.py
LOGIN_REDIRECT_URL = "home"   # new
LOGOUT_REDIRECT_URL = "home"   # new
```

Now we can create four new templates within our text editor:

- templates/base.html
- templates/home.html
- templates/registration/login.html
- templates/registration/signup.html

Here's the HTML code for each file to use. The base.html will be inherited by every other template in our project. By using a block like {% block content %} we can later override the content *just in this place* in other templates.

Code

```
<!-- templates/base.html -->
<!DOCTYPE html>
<html>
<head>
  <meta charset="utf-8">
  <title>{% block title %}Newspaper App{% endblock title %}</title>
</head>
<body>
  <main>
    {% block content %}
    {% endblock content %}
  </main>
</body>
</html>
```

Code

```
<!-- templates/home.html -->
{% extends "base.html" %}

{% block title %}Home{% endblock title %}

{% block content %}
{% if user.is_authenticated %}
  Hi {{ user.username }}!
  <p><a href="{% url 'logout' %}">Log Out</a></p>
{% else %}
  <p>You are not logged in</p>
  <a href="{% url 'login' %}">Log In</a> |
  <a href="{% url 'signup' %}">Sign Up</a>
{% endif %}
{% endblock content %}
```

Code

```
<!-- templates/registration/login.html -->
{% extends "base.html" %}

{% block title %}Log In{% endblock title %}

{% block content %}
<h2>Log In</h2>
<form method="post">{% csrf_token %}
  {{ form.as_p }}
  <button type="submit">Log In</button>
</form>
{% endblock content %}
```

Code

```
<!-- templates/registration/signup.html -->
{% extends "base.html" %}

{% block title %}Sign Up{% endblock title %}

{% block content %}
<h2>Sign Up</h2>
<form method="post">{% csrf_token %}
  {{ form.as_p }}
  <button type="submit">Sign Up</button>
</form>
{% endblock content %}
```

Our templates are now all set. Still to go are the related URLs and views.

URLs

Let's start with the URL routes. In our `django_project/urls.py` file, we want to have our `home.html` template appear as the homepage, but we don't want to build a dedicated `pages` app just yet. We can use the shortcut of importing `TemplateView` and setting the `template_name` right in our url pattern.

Next, we want to "include" both the `accounts` app and the built-in `auth` app. The reason is that the built-in `auth` app already provides views and urls for log in and log out. But for sign up we will need to create our own view and url. To ensure that our URL routes are consistent we place them *both* at accounts/ so the eventual URLS will be /accounts/login, /accounts/logout, and /accounts/signup.

Code

```
# django_project/urls.py
from django.contrib import admin
from django.urls import path, include  # new
from django.views.generic.base import TemplateView  # new

urlpatterns = [
    path("admin/", admin.site.urls),
    path("accounts/", include("accounts.urls")),  # new
    path("accounts/", include("django.contrib.auth.urls")),  # new
    path("", TemplateView.as_view(template_name="home.html"),
      name="home"),  # new
]
```

Now create a file with your text editor called accounts/urls.py and update it with the following code:

Code

```
# accounts/urls.py
from django.urls import path
from .views import SignUpView

urlpatterns = [
    path("signup/", SignUpView.as_view(), name="signup"),
]
```

The last step is our views.py file which will contain the logic for our sign up form. We're using Django's generic CreateView here and telling it to use our CustomUserCreationForm, to redirect to login once a user signs up successfully, and that our template is named signup.html.

Code

```python
# accounts/views.py
from django.urls import reverse_lazy
from django.views.generic import CreateView

from .forms import CustomUserCreationForm


class SignUpView(CreateView):
    form_class = CustomUserCreationForm
    success_url = reverse_lazy('login')
    template_name = "registration/signup.html"
```

Ok, phew! We're done. Let's test things out. Start up the server with `python manage.py runserver` and go to the homepage.

Homepage logged in

We logged in to the admin in the previous chapter so you should see a personalized greeting here. Click on the "Log Out" link.

Homepage logged out

Now we're on the logged out homepage. Go ahead and click on *Log In* link and use your **superuser** credentials.

Log in

Upon successfully logging in you'll be redirected back to the homepage and see the same personalized greeting. It works! Now use the "Log Out" link to return to the homepage and this time click on the "Sign Up" link. You'll be redirected to our signup page. See that the age field is included!

Create a new user. Mine is called testuser and I've set the age to 25.

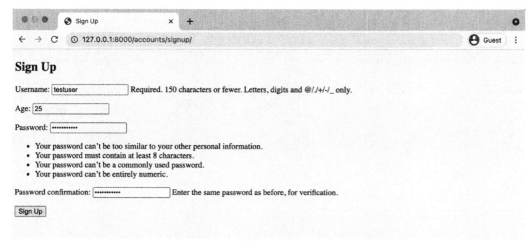

Sign up page

After successfully submitting the form you'll be redirected to the log in page. Log in with your new user and you'll again be redirected to the homepage with a personalized greeting for the new user. But since we have the new age field, let's add that to the home.html template. It is a field on the user model, so to display it we only need to use {{ user.age }}.

Code

```
<!-- templates/home.html -->
{% extends "base.html" %}

{% block title %}Home{% endblock title %}

{% block content %}
{% if user.is_authenticated %}
  Hi {{ user.username }}! You are {{ user.age }} years old.
  <p><a href="{% url 'logout' %}">Log Out</a></p>
{% else %}
  <p>You are not logged in</p>
  <a href="{% url 'login' %}">Log In</a> |
  <a href="{% url 'signup' %}">Sign Up</a>
{% endif %}
{% endblock content %}
```

Save the file and refresh the homepage.

Homepage for testuser

Everything works as expected.

Admin

Navigate to the admin at http://127.0.0.1:8000/admin in your web browser and then log in to view the two user accounts.

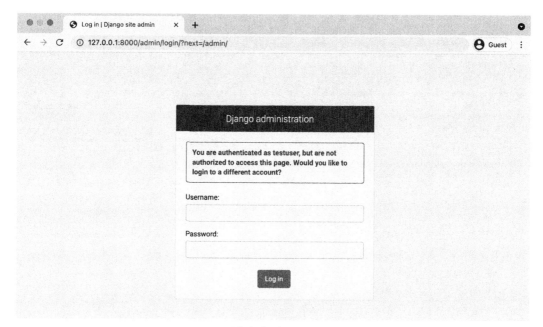

Admin log in wrong

What's this! Why can't we log in? Well we're logged in with our new `testuser` account not our superuser account. Only a superuser account has the permissions to log in to the admin! So use your superuser account to log in instead.

After you've done that you should see the normal admin homepage. Click on `Users` and you can see our two users: the `testuser` account we just created and your previous superuser name (mine is `wsv`).

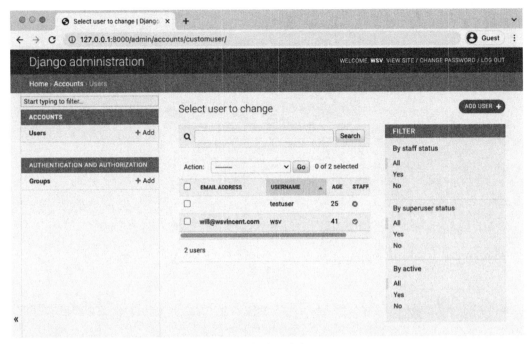

Users in the Admin

Everything is working but you may notice that there is no "Email address" for our `testuser`. Why is that? Well, our sign up page has no email field because it was not included in `accounts/forms.py`. This is an important point: just because the `user` model has a field does not mean it will be included in our custom sign up form unless it is explicitly added. Let's do so now.

Currently, in `accounts/forms.py` under `fields` we're using `Meta.fields`, which just displays the default settings of username/age/password. But we can also explicitly set which fields we want displayed so let's update it to ask for a username/email/age/password by setting it to `('username', 'email', 'age',)`. We don't need to include the `password` fields because they are required! All the other fields can be configured however we choose.

Code

```python
# accounts/forms.py
from django.contrib.auth.forms import UserCreationForm, UserChangeForm

from .models import CustomUser


class CustomUserCreationForm(UserCreationForm):
    class Meta(UserCreationForm):
        model = CustomUser
        fields = (
            "username",
            "email",
            "age",
        )  # new


class CustomUserChangeForm(UserChangeForm):
    class Meta:
        model = CustomUser
        fields = (
            "username",
            "email",
            "age",
        )  # new
```

Now if you try http://127.0.0.1:8000/accounts/signup/ again you can see the additional "Email address" field is there.

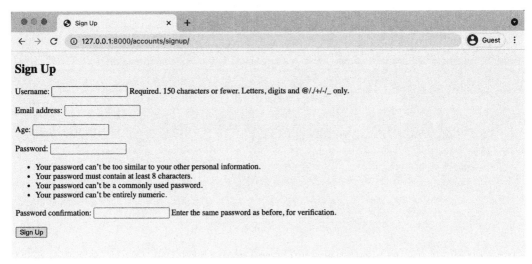

New sign up page

Sign up with a new user account. I've named mine `testuser2` with an age of `18` and an email address of `testuser2@email.com`. Continue to log in and you'll see a personalized greeting on the homepage.

testuser2 homepage greeting

Then switch back to the admin page–log in using our superuser account to do so–and all three users are on display. Note that I've closed the side nav bar of the admin in this screenshot by clicking on the arrows >> to make it more readable.

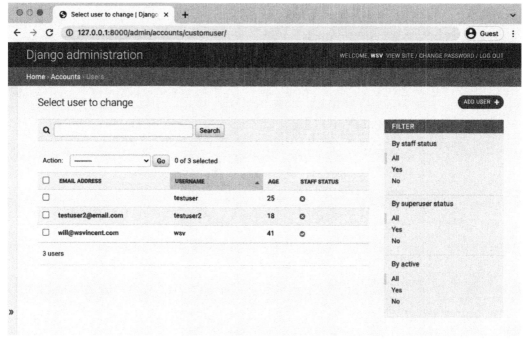

Three users in the Admin

Django's user authentication flow requires a little bit of set up but you should be starting to see that it also provides us incredible flexibility to configure sign up and log in *exactly* how we want.

Tests

The new sign up page has its own view, URL, and template which should all be tested. Open up the accounts/tests.py file and add the following code which we will review below.

Code

```python
# accounts/tests.py
from django.contrib.auth import get_user_model
from django.test import TestCase
from django.urls import reverse


class SignupPageTests(TestCase):
    def test_url_exists_at_correct_location_signupview(self):
        response = self.client.get("/accounts/signup/")
        self.assertEqual(response.status_code, 200)

    def test_signup_view_name(self):
        response = self.client.get(reverse("signup"))
        self.assertEqual(response.status_code, 200)
        self.assertTemplateUsed(response, "registration/signup.html")

    def test_signup_form(self):
        response = self.client.post(
            reverse("signup"),
            {
                "username": "testuser",
                "email": "testuser@email.com",
                "password1": "testpass123",
                "password2": "testpass123",
            },
        )
        self.assertEqual(response.status_code, 302)
        self.assertEqual(get_user_model().objects.all().count(), 1)
        self.assertEqual(get_user_model().objects.all()[0].username, "testuser")
        self.assertEqual(get_user_model().objects.all()[0].email, "testuser@email.com")
```

At the top we import get_user_model()[123] so we can test our sign up form. Then we also import
TestCase to run tests that touch the database and reverse so we can verify the URL and view
work properly.

Our class of tests is called SignupPageTests and extends TestCase. The first test checks that our
sign up page is at the correct URL and returns a 200 status code. The second test checks the view.
It reverses signup which is the URL name, confirms a 200 status code, and that our signup.html
template is being used.

---

[123]https://docs.djangoproject.com/en/4.0/topics/auth/customizing/#django.contrib.auth.get_user_model

The third test checks our form by sending a `post` request to fill it out. We expect a `302` redirect after the form is submitted and then confirm that there is now one user in the test database with a matching username and email address. We do not check the password because Django automatically encrypts them by default. That is why if you look in the admin view of a user you can change a password but you can't see what the current one actually is.

Run the tests with `python manage.py test` to check that everything passes as expected.

Shell

```
(.venv) > python manage.py test
Found 3 test(s).
Creating test database for alias 'default'...
System check identified no issues (0 silenced).
...
-------------------------------------------------------------------
Ran 3 tests in 0.183s

OK
Destroying test database for alias 'default'...
```

Conclusion

So far our *Newspaper* app has a custom user model and working sign up, log in, and log out pages. But you may have noticed our site doesn't look very good. In the next chapter we'll add styling with Bootstrap and create a dedicated `pages` app.

Chapter 10: Bootstrap

Web development requires a lot of skills. Not only do you have to program the website to work correctly, users expect it to look good, too. When you're creating everything from scratch, it can be overwhelming to also add all the necessary HTML/CSS for a beautiful site.

While it's possible to hand-code all the required CSS and JavaScript for a modern-looking website, in practice most developers user a framework like Bootstrap[124] or TailwindCSS[125]. For our project, we'll use Bootstrap which can be extended and customized as needed.

Pages App

In the previous chapter we displayed our homepage by including view logic in our `urls.py` file. While this approach works, it feels somewhat hackish to me and it certainly doesn't scale as a website grows over time. It is also probably somewhat confusing to Django newcomers. Instead, we can and should create a dedicated `pages` app for all our static pages, such as the homepage, a future about page, and so on. This will keep our code nice and organized going forward.

On the command line ,use the `startapp` command to create our new `pages` app. If the server is still running you may need to type `Control+c` first to quit it.

Shell

```
(.venv) > python manage.py startapp pages
```

Then immediately update our `django_project/settings.py` file. I often forget to do this so it is a good practice to just think of creating a new app as a two-step process: run the `startapp` command then update `INSTALLED_APPS`.

---

[124]https://getbootstrap.com/
[125]https://tailwindcss.com/

Code

```
# django_project/settings.py
INSTALLED_APPS = [
    "django.contrib.admin",
    "django.contrib.auth",
    "django.contrib.contenttypes",
    "django.contrib.sessions",
    "django.contrib.messages",
    "django.contrib.staticfiles",
    "accounts.apps.AccountsConfig",
    "pages.apps.PagesConfig",  # new
]
```

Now we can update our `urls.py` file inside the `django_project` directory by adding the `pages` app, removing the import of `TemplateView`, and removing the previous URL path for the older homepage.

Code

```
# django_project/urls.py
from django.contrib import admin
from django.urls import path, include

urlpatterns = [
    path("admin/", admin.site.urls),
    path("accounts/", include("accounts.urls")),
    path("accounts/", include("django.contrib.auth.urls")),
    path("", include("pages.urls")),  # new
]
```

It's time to add our homepage which means Django's standard urls/views/templates dance. We'll start with the `pages/urls.py` file. First create it with your text editor. Then import our not-yet-created views, set the route paths, and make sure to name each url, too.

Code

```
# pages/urls.py
from django.urls import path

from .views import HomePageView

urlpatterns = [
    path("", HomePageView.as_view(), name="home"),
]
```

The `views.py` code should look familiar at this point. We're using Django's `TemplateView` generic class-based view which means we only need to specify our `template_name` to use it.

Code

```
# pages/views.py
from django.views.generic import TemplateView


class HomePageView(TemplateView):
    template_name = "home.html"
```

We already have an existing `home.html` template. Let's confirm it still works as expected with our new url and view. Start up the local server `python manage.py runserver` and navigate to the homepage at `http://127.0.0.1:8000/` to confirm it remains unchanged.

Homepage logged in

It should show the name and age of your logged in superuser account which we used at the end of the last chapter.

Tests

We've added new code and functionality which means it is time for tests. You can never have enough tests in your projects. Even though they take some upfront time to write, they always save you time down the road and give confidence as a project grows in complexity.

Let's add tests to ensure our new homepage works properly. Here's what the code should look like in your pages/tests.py file.

Code

```python
# pages/tests.py
from django.test import SimpleTestCase
from django.urls import reverse


class HomePageTests(SimpleTestCase):
    def test_url_exists_at_correct_location_homepageview(self):
        response = self.client.get("/")
        self.assertEqual(response.status_code, 200)

    def test_homepage_view(self):
        response = self.client.get(reverse("home"))
        self.assertEqual(response.status_code, 200)
        self.assertTemplateUsed(response, "home.html")
        self.assertContains(response, "Home")
```

On the top line we import SimpleTestCase since our homepage does not rely on the database. If it did we'd have to use TestCase instead. Then we import reverse to test our URL and view.

Our test class, HomePageTests, has two tests that check the homepage URL returns a 200 status code and that it uses our expected URL name, template, and contains "Home" in the response.

Quit the local server with Control+c and then run our tests to confirm everything passes.

Shell

```
(.venv) > python manage.py test
Creating test database for alias 'default'...
System check identified no issues (0 silenced).
.......
----------------------------------------------------------------------
Ran 5 tests in 0.185s

OK
Destroying test database for alias 'default'...
```

Testing Philosophy

There's really no limit to what you can test in an application. For example, we *could* also add tests now based on logged-in or logged-out behavior and whether the template displays the proper content. But the 80/20 rule of 80% of consequences coming from 20% of causes applies to testing as well as most other things in life. There's no sense making as many unit tests as possible to test things that will likely never fail, at least for a web application. If we were working on a nuclear reactor then it would make sense to have as many tests as possible, but the stakes are a bit lower for most websites.

So while you do always want to add tests around new features, it's ok to not have complete test coverage from the beginning. As errors inevitably arise on new Git branches and features, make sure to add a test for each so they don't fail again. This is known as regression testing where tests are re-run each time there's a new change to ensure that previously developed and tested software performs as expected.

Django's testing suite is well setup for many unit tests and automatic regression tests so developers have confidence in the consistency of their projects.

Bootstrap

Moving along now it's time to add some style to our application. If you've never used Bootstrap before you're in for a real treat. Much like Django, it accomplishes so much in so little code.

There are two ways to add Bootstrap to a project: you can download all the files and serve them locally or rely on a Content Delivery Network (CDN). The second approach is simpler to implement provided you have a consistent internet connection so that's what we'll use here.

Our template will mimic the "Starter template" provided on the Bootstrap introduction[126] page and involves adding the following:

- `meta name="viewport"` at the top within `<head>`
- also adding Bootstrap CSS link within `<head>`
- adding Bootstrap JavaScript bundle at the bottom of the `<body>` section

In general, typing out all code yourself is the recommended approach but adding the Bootstrap CDN is an exception since it is lengthy and easy to miss-type. I recommend copy and pasting the Bootstrap CSS and JavaScript Bundle links from the website into the `base.html` file.

Code

```
<!-- templates/base.html -->
<!DOCTYPE html>
<html>
<head>
  <meta charset="utf-8">
  <title>{% block title %}Newspaper App{% endblock title %}</title>
  <meta name="viewport" content="width=device-width,
  initial-scale=1, shrink-to-fit=no">

  <!-- Bootstrap CSS -->
  <link href="https://cdn.jsdelivr.net/npm/bootstrap@5.1.1..." rel="stylesheet">
</head>
<body>
  <main>
    {% block content %}
    {% endblock content %}
  </main>

  <!-- Bootstrap JavaScript Bundle -->
  <script src="https://cdn.jsdelivr.net/npm/bootstrap@5.1.1..."></script>
</body>
</html>
```

[126]https://getbootstrap.com/docs/5.1/getting-started/introduction/

This code snippet **does not** include the full links for Bootstrap CSS and JavaScript. It is abbreviated. Copy and paste the full links for Bootstrap 5.1 from the quick start docs[127].

If you start the server again with `python manage.py runserver` and refresh the homepage at `http://127.0.0.1:8000/` you'll see that the font size has changed as well as the link colors.

Let's add a navigation bar at the top of the page which contains our links for the homepage, log in, log out, and sign up. Notably, we can use the if/else[128] tags in the Django templating engine to add some basic logic. We want to show a "log in" and "sign up" button to users who are logged out, but a "log out" and "change password" button to users logged in.

Again, it's ok to copy/paste here since the focus of this book is on learning Django not HTML, CSS, and Bootstrap. If there are any formatting issues you can view the source code online[129].

Code

```
<!-- templates/base.html -->
...
<body>
<div class="container">
  <header class="p-3 mb-3 border-bottom">
    <div class="container">
      <div class="d-flex flex-wrap align-items-center justify-content-center
        justify-content-lg-start">
        <a class="navbar-brand" href="{% url 'home' %}">Newspaper</a>
        <ul class="nav col-12 col-lg-auto me-lg-auto mb-2 justify-content-center
          mb-md-0">
        {% if user.is_authenticated %}
          <li><a href="#" class="nav-link px-2 link-dark">+ New</a></li>
        </ul>
        <div class="dropdown text-end">
          <a href="#" class="d-block link-dark text-decoration-none dropdown-toggle"
            id="dropdownUser1" data-bs-toggle="dropdown" aria-expanded="false">
            {{ user.username }}
          </a>
          <ul class="dropdown-menu text-small" aria-labelledby="dropdownUser1">
            <li><a class="dropdown-item" href="{% url 'password_change'%}">
              Change password</a></li>
            <li><a class="dropdown-item" href="{% url 'logout' %}">Log Out</a></li>
          </ul>
```

---

[127]https://getbootstrap.com/docs/5.1/getting-started/introduction/#quick-start
[128]https://docs.djangoproject.com/en/4.0/ref/templates/language/#tags
[129]https://github.com/wsvincent/djangoforbeginners

```
      </div>
      {% else %}
      </ul>
      <div class="text-end">
        <a href="{% url 'login' %}" class="btn btn-outline-primary me-2">
          Log In</a>
        <a href="{% url 'signup' %}" class="btn btn-primary">Sign Up</a>
      </div>
      {% endif %}
    </div>
  </div>
</header>

<main>
  {% block content %}
  {% endblock content %}
</main>
</div>
...
```

If you refresh the homepage at http://127.0.0.1:8000/ our new nav has magically appeared!
Note that the link for new articles "+ New" does not have a link yet as represented by href="".
We will add that later on. Also note that our logged-in username is now in the upper right corner
along with a dropdown arrow. If you click on it, there are links for "Change password" and "Log
Out."

If you click on the "Log Out" in the dropdown the nav bar changes to button links for either
"Log In" or "Sign Up" and the "+ New" link disappears. No sense in letting logged out users create
articles.

Homepage with Bootstrap nav logged out

If you click on the "Log In" button from the top nav you can also see that our log in page `http://127.0.0.1:8000/accounts/login` looks better too.

Bootstrap login

The only thing that looks off is our "Login" button. We can use Bootstrap to add some nice styling such as making it green and inviting.

Change the "button" line in `templates/registration/login.html` as follows.

Code

```
<!-- templates/registration/login.html -->
{% extends "base.html" %}

{% block title %}Log In{% endblock title %}

{% block content %}
<h2>Log In</h2>
<form method="post">{% csrf_token %}
  {{ form.as_p }}
  <button class="btn btn-success ml-2" type="submit">Log In</button>
</form>
{% endblock content %}
```

Now refresh the page to see our new button in action.

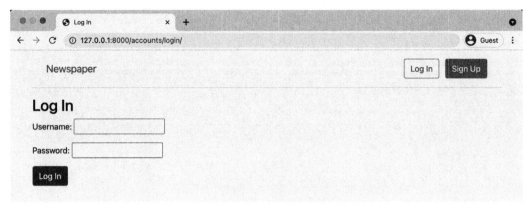

Bootstrap log in with new button

Sign Up Form

If you click on the link for "Sign Up" you'll see that the page has Bootstrap stylings but also distracting helper text. For example after "Username" it says "Required. 150 characters or fewer. Letters, digits and @/./+/-/_ only."

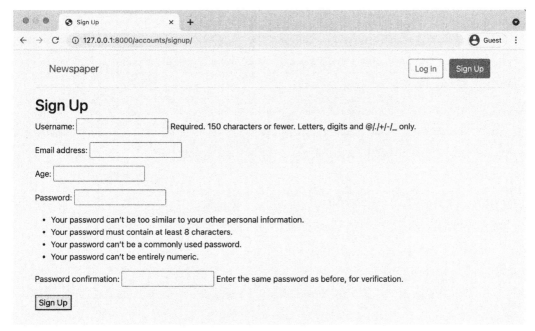

Updated navbar logged out

Where did that text come from, right? Whenever something feels like "magic" in Django rest assured that it is decidedly not. Likely the code came from an internal piece of Django.

The fastest method I've found to figure out what's happening under-the-hood in Django is to simply go to the Django source code on GitHub[130], use the search bar and try to find the specific piece of text.

For example, if you do a search for "150 characters or fewer" you'll find yourself on the page for `django/contrib/auth/models.py`. As of this writing, this is the link[131] and the specific line is on line 334. The text comes as part of the `auth` app, on the `username` field for `AbstractUser`.

We have three options now:

- override the existing `help_text`
- hide the `help_text`

---

[130]https://github.com/django/django

[131]https://github.com/django/django/blob/7af8f4127397279d19ef7c7899e93018274e2f9b/django/contrib/auth/models.py

- restyle the `help_text`

We'll choose the third option since it's a good way to introduce the excellent 3rd party package django-crispy-forms[132].

Working with forms is a challenge and `django-crispy-forms` makes it easier to write DRY (Don't-Repeat-Yourself) code. First, stop the local server with `Control+c`. Then use `pip` to install the package in our project. We'll also install the Bootstrap5 template pack[133].

Shell

```
(.venv) > python -m pip install django-crispy-forms==1.13.0
(.venv) > python -m pip install crispy-bootstrap5==0.6
```

Add the new apps to our `INSTALLED_APPS` list in the `django_project/settings.py` file. As the number of apps starts to grow, I find it helpful to distinguish between 3rd party apps and local apps I've added myself. Here's what the code looks like now.

Code

```python
# django_project/settings.py
INSTALLED_APPS = [
    "django.contrib.admin",
    "django.contrib.auth",
    "django.contrib.contenttypes",
    "django.contrib.sessions",
    "django.contrib.messages",
    "django.contrib.staticfiles",
    # 3rd Party
    "crispy_forms",  # new
    "crispy_bootstrap5",  # new
    # Local
    "accounts.apps.AccountsConfig",
    "pages.apps.PagesConfig",
]
```

And then at the bottom of the `settings.py` file add two new lines as well.

---

[132]https://github.com/django-crispy-forms/django-crispy-forms
[133]https://github.com/django-crispy-forms/crispy-bootstrap5

Code

```
# django_project/settings.py
CRISPY_ALLOWED_TEMPLATE_PACKS = "bootstrap5"  # new
CRISPY_TEMPLATE_PACK = "bootstrap5"  # new
```

Now in our `signup.html` template we can quickly use crispy forms. First, we load `crispy_forms_-tags` at the top and then swap out `{{ form.as_p }}` for `{{ form|crispy }}`. We'll also update the "Sign Up" button to be green with the `btn-success` styling.

Code

```
<!-- templates/registration/signup.html -->
{% extends "base.html" %}
{% load crispy_forms_tags %}
{% block title %}Sign Up{% endblock title%}

{% block content %}
<h2>Sign Up</h2>
<form method="post">{% csrf_token %}
    {{ form|crispy }}
    <button class="btn btn-success" type="submit">Sign Up</button>
  </form>
{% endblock content %}
```

If you start up the server again with `python manage.py runserver` and refresh the sign up page we can see the new changes.

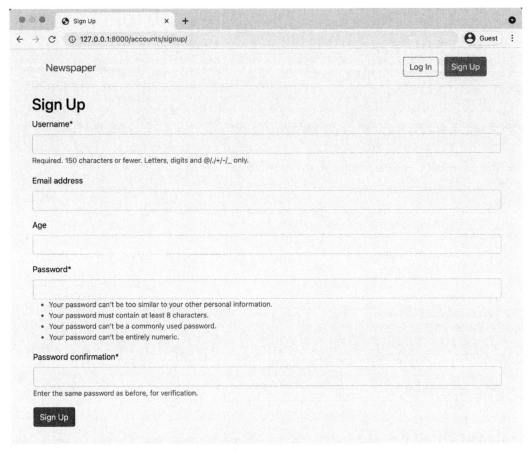

Crispy sign up page

We can also add crispy forms to our log in page. The process is the same. Here is that updated code:

Code

```
<!-- templates/registration/login.html -->
{% extends "base.html" %}
{% load crispy_forms_tags %}

{% block title %}Log In{% endblock title %}

{% block content %}
<h2>Log In</h2>
<form method="post">{% csrf_token %}
  {{ form|crispy }}
  <button class="btn btn-success ml-2" type="submit">Log In</button>
</form>
{% endblock content %}
```

Refresh the log in page and the update will be visible.

Crispy log in page

Conclusion

Our *Newspaper* app is starting to look pretty good. We added Bootstrap to our site as well as Django Crispy Forms to improve the look of our forms. The last step of our user auth flow is to configure password change and reset. Here again Django has taken care of the heavy lifting so it requires a minimal amount of code on our part.

Chapter 11: Password Change and Reset

In this chapter we will complete the authorization flow of our *Newspaper* app by adding password change and password reset functionality. Initially we will implement Django's built-in views and URLs for both password change and password reset before then customizing them with our own Bootstrap-powered templates and email service.

Password Change

Letting users change their passwords is a common feature on many websites. Django provides a default implementation that already works at this stage. To try it out first click on the "Log In" button to make sure you're logged in. Then navigate to the "Password change" page, which is located at `http://127.0.0.1:8000/accounts/password_change/`.

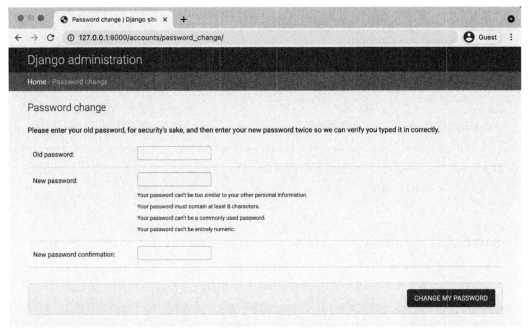

Password change

Enter in both your old password and a new one. Then click the "Change My Password" button. You will be redirected to the "Password change successful" page.

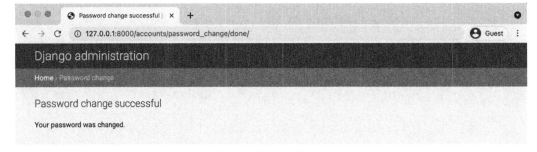

Password change done

Customizing Password Change

Let's customize these two password change pages so that they match the look and feel of our *Newspaper* site. Because Django already has created the views and URLs for us we only need to change the templates. In your text editor create two new template files in the `registration` directory:

- `templates/registration/password_change_form.html`
- `templates/registration/password_change_done.html`

Update `password_change_form.html` with the following code. At the top we extend `base.html`, load crispy forms, and set our page meta title. This is what appears in the tab of a web browser but not on the visible webpage itself. The form uses `POST` since we're sending data, a `csrf_token` for security reasons, and `{{ form|crispy }}` to use crispy forms styling. As a final tweak, we include a submit button that uses Bootstrap's `btn btn-success` styling to make it green.

Code

```
<!-- templates/registration/password_change_form.html -->
{% extends "base.html" %}
{% load crispy_forms_tags %}

{% block title %}Password Change{% endblock title %}

{% block content %}
<h1>Password change</h1>
<p>Please enter your old password, for security's sake, and then enter
your new password twice so we can verify you typed it in correctly.</p>

<form method="POST">{% csrf_token %}
  {{ form|crispy }}
  <input class="btn btn-success" type="submit"
    value="Change my password">
</form>
{% endblock content %}
```

Go ahead and load the page at `http://127.0.0.1:8000/accounts/password_change/)` to see our changes.

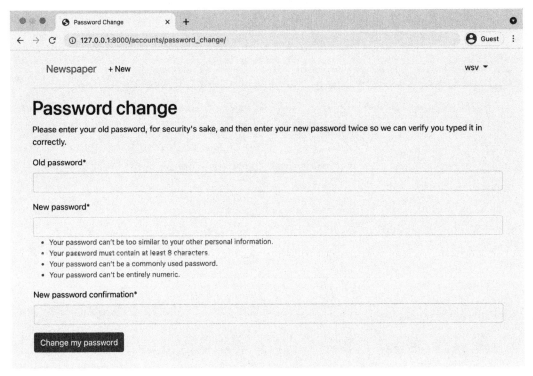

New password change form

Next up is the `password_change_done` template. It also extends `base.html` and includes a new meta title however there's no form on the page, just new text.

Code

```
<!-- templates/registration/password_change_done.html -->
{% extends "base.html" %}

{% block title %}Password Change Successful{% endblock title %}

{% block content %}
  <h1>Password change successful</h1>
  <p>Your password was changed.</p>
{% endblock content %}
```

This updated page is at:

```
http://127.0.0.1:8000/accounts/password_change/done/
```

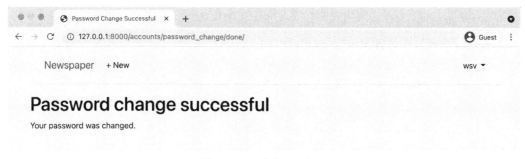

New password change done

That wasn't too bad, right? Certainly it was a lot less work than creating everything from scratch, especially all the code around securely updating a user's password. Next up is the password reset functionality.

Password Reset

Password reset handles the common case of users forgetting their passwords. The steps are very similar to configuring password change, as we just did. Django already provides a default implementation that we will use and then customize the templates so it matches the look and feel of the rest of our site.

The only configuration required is telling Django *how* to send emails. After all, a user can only reset a password if they have access to the email linked to the account. In production, we'll use the email service SendGrid to actually send the emails but for testing purposes we can rely on Django's console backend[134] setting which outputs the email text to our command line console instead.

At the bottom of the `django_project/settings.py` file add the following one-line change.

---

[134]https://docs.djangoproject.com/en/4.0/topics/email/#console-backend

Code

```
# django_project/settings.py
EMAIL_BACKEND = "django.core.mail.backends.console.EmailBackend"  # new
```

And we're all set! Django will take care of all the rest for us. Let's try it out. Navigate to `http://127.0.0.1:8000/accounts/password_reset/` to view the default password reset page.

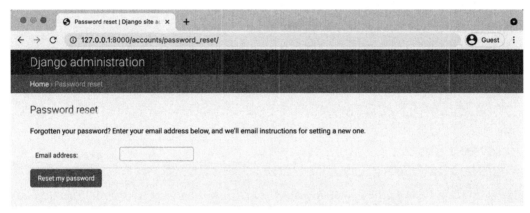

Default password reset page

Make sure the email address you enter matches one of your existing user accounts. Recall that `testuser` does not have a linked email account so you should use `testuser2` which, if you followed my example, has an email address of `testuser2@email.com`. Upon submission you'll then be redirected to the password reset done page at:

`http://127.0.0.1:8000/accounts/password_reset/done/`

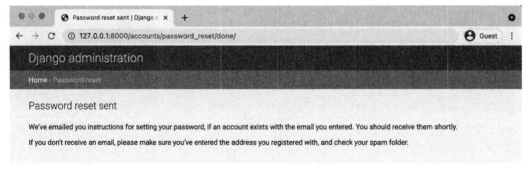

Default password reset done page

This page says to check our email. Since we've told Django to send emails to the command line console, the email text will now be there. This is what I see in my console.

Shell

```
Content-Type: text/plain; charset="utf-8"
MIME-Version: 1.0
Content-Transfer-Encoding: 8bit
Subject: Password reset on 127.0.0.1:8000
From: webmaster@localhost
To: testuser2@email.com
Date: Fri, 10 Dec 2021 14:04:57 -0000
Message-ID: <163422029788.81248.2976605416677047926@1.0.0.127.in-addr.arpa>


You're receiving this email because you requested a password reset for your user
account at 127.0.0.1:8000.

Please go to the following page and choose a new password:

http://127.0.0.1:8000/accounts/reset/Mw/auihs9-ed00b2be2d\
2f9cb5fbb71d42764d9ddd/

Your username, in case you've forgotten: testuser2

Thanks for using our site!

The 127.0.0.1:8000 team

------------------------------------------------------------------------
[10/Dec/2021 14:04:57] "POST /accounts/password_reset/ HTTP/1.1" 302 0
[10/Dec/2021 14:04:57] "GET /accounts/password_reset/done/ HTTP/1.1" 200 1583
```

Your email text should be identical except for three lines:

- the "To" on the sixth line contains the email address of the user
- the URL link contains a secure token that Django randomly generates for us and can be used only once
- Django helpfully reminds us of our username

We will customize all of the email default text shortly but for now focus on finding the link provided and enter it into your web browser and you'll be redirected to the "Password reset confirmation" page.

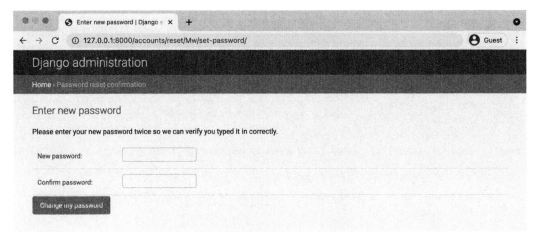

Default password reset confirmation

Now enter in a new password and click on the "Change my password" button. The final step is you'll be redirected to the "Password reset complete" page.

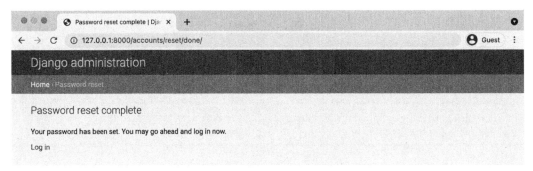

Default password reset complete

To confirm everything worked, click on the "Log in" link and use your new password. It should work.

Custom Templates

As with the Password Change pages we can create new templates to customize the look and feel of the entire password reset flow. If you noticed, there are four separate templates used. Create these new files now in your `templates/registration/` directory.

- `templates/registration/password_reset_form.html`
- `templates/registration/password_reset_done.html`
- `templates/registration/password_reset_confirm.html`
- `templates/registration/password_reset_complete.html`

Start with the password reset form which is `password_reset_form.html`. At the top we extend `base.html`, load `crispy_forms_tags`, and set the meta page title. Because we used "block" titles in our `base.html` file we can override them here. The form uses `POST` since we're sending data, a `csrf_token` for security reasons, and `{{ form|crispy }}` for the forms. And we again update the submit button to be green. At this point the process of updating these template pages should start to feel somewhat familiar.

Code

```
<!-- templates/registration/password_reset_form.html -->
{% extends "base.html" %}
{% load crispy_forms_tags %}

{% block title %}Forgot Your Password?{% endblock title %}

{% block content %}
<h1>Forgot your password?</h1>
<p>Enter your email address below, and we'll email instructions
for setting a new one.</p>

<form method="POST">{% csrf_token %}
  {{ form|crispy }}
  <input class="btn btn-success" type="submit"
    value="Send me instructions!">
</form>
{% endblock content %}
```

Start up the server again with `python manage.py runserver` and navigate to:

`http://127.0.0.1:8000/accounts/password_reset/`

Refresh the page you can see our new page.

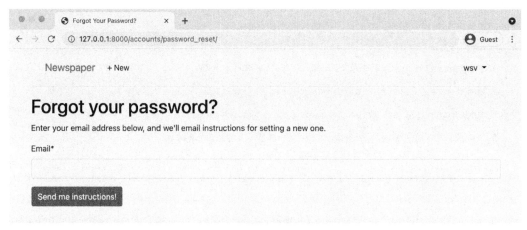

New password reset

Now we can update the other three pages. Each takes the same form of extending `base.html`, setting a new meta title, and adding new content text. When there is a form involved we switch to loading and using crispy forms.

Let's begin with the `password_reset_done.html` template.

Code

```
<!-- templates/registration/password_reset_done.html -->
{% extends "base.html" %}

{% block title %}Email Sent{% endblock title %}

{% block content %}
<h1>Check your inbox.</h1>
<p>We've emailed you instructions for setting your password.
You should receive the email shortly!</p>
{% endblock content %}
```

Confirm the changes by going to `http://127.0.0.1:8000/accounts/password_reset/done/`.

New reset done

Next up is `password_reset_confirm.html`. Note that it has a form so we'll use crispy forms here.

Code

```
<!-- templates/registration/password_reset_confirm.html -->
{% extends "base.html" %}
{% load crispy_forms_tags %}

{% block title %}Enter new password{% endblock title %}

{% block content %}
<h1>Set a new password!</h1>
<form method="POST">{% csrf_token %}
  {{ form|crispy }}
  <input class="btn btn-success" type="submit" value="Change my password">
</form>
{% endblock content %}
```

In the command line grab the URL link from the email outputted to the console and you'll see the following.

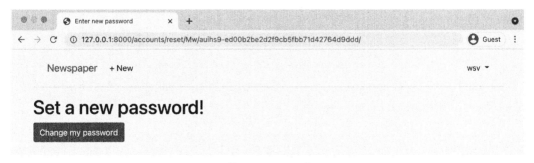

New set password

Finally here is the password reset complete code.

Code

```
<!-- templates/registration/password_reset_complete.html -->
{% extends "base.html" %}

{% block title %}Password reset complete{% endblock title %}

{% block content %}
<h1>Password reset complete</h1>
<p>Your new password has been set.</p>
<p>You can log in now on the
<a href="{% url 'login' %}">Log In page</a>.</p>
{% endblock content %}
```

You can view it at `http://127.0.0.1:8000/accounts/reset/done/`.

New password reset complete

Try It Out

Let's confirm everything is working by resetting the password for the `testuser2` account. Log out of your current account and head to the Log In page. This is the logical location for a "Forgot your password?" link that sends a user into the password reset section. Let's add that link now.

Code

```
<!-- templates/registration/login.html -->
{% extends "base.html" %}
{% load crispy_forms_tags %}

{% block title %}Log In{% endblock title %}

{% block content %}
<h2>Log In</h2>
<form method="post">{% csrf_token %}
  {{ form|crispy }}
  <button class="btn btn-success ml-2" type="submit">Log In</button>
</form>
<p><a href="{% url 'password_reset' %}">Forgot your password?</a></p>
{% endblock content %}
```

First we'll need to add the password reset link to the existing Log In page since we can't assume the user will know the correct URL! That goes on the bottom of the form. Refresh the webpage for log in to confirm it is there.

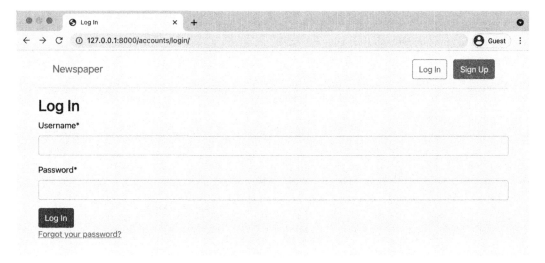

Forgot Your Password link

Click on the link to bring up the Password Reset template and complete the flow by using the email for `testuser2@email.com`. Remember that the unique link will be outputted to your console. Set a new password and use it to log in to the `testuser2` account.

Conclusion

In the next chapter we will connect our *Newspaper* app to the email service SendGrid so our automated emails are actually sent to users as opposed to outputting them in the command line console.

Chapter 12: Email

At this point you may be feeling a little overwhelmed by all the user authentication configuration we've done up to this point. That's normal. After all, we haven't even created any core *Newspaper* app features yet! Everything has been about setting up custom user accounts and the rest.

The upside to Django's approach is that it is incredibly easy to customize any piece of our website. The downside is that Django requires a bit more out-of-the-box code than some competing web frameworks. As you become more and more experienced in web development, the wisdom of Django's approach will ring true.

Currently, emails are outputted to our command line console. They are not actually sent to users. Let's change that! First we need to sign up for an account at SendGrid[135] as our email provider. Then update the `django_project/settings.py` files and Django will take care of the rest. Ready?

SendGrid

SendGrid is a popular service for sending transactional emails so we'll use it. Django doesn't care what service you choose though. The steps taken here will be almost identical to what you'll need with any other email service provider.

On the SendGrid website sign up for a free account. Make sure that the email account you use for SendGrid **is not** the same email account you have for your superuser account on the *Newspaper* project or weird errors may result. On the "Tell Us About Yourself" page is a required field for "Company Website". I recommend using the URL of your Heroku deployment from a previous chapter here as this setting can later be changed. Then on the bottom of the page click the "Get Started" button.

SendGrid then presents us with a welcome screen and a prompt to "Create a Single Sender". This approach is far faster for verifying that our website and emails work correctly. For a production website taking the additional steps to authenticate your domain is recommended instead.

---

[135]https://sendgrid.com/

After clicking on the "Create a Single Sender" button you are brought to a "Create a Sender" page. It requires entering a name, email, and physical address. These are all requirements that help to minimize email spam and are now required in most countries. Note that you should use a real email address here because SendGrid will send a verification email link to it.

Check your email and click on the link to "Verify Single Sender" from SendGrid. It will redirect to a "Sender Verified" page and has a link to "Return to Single Sender Verification".

To send our first email, there should be a prompt at the top of the page at this point. If not, you can go directly to the guide at `https://app.sendgrid.com/guide`.

SendGrid offers two main ways to send our first email. Select the first option for "Integrate using our Web API or SMTP relay" and click on the "Start" button next to it.

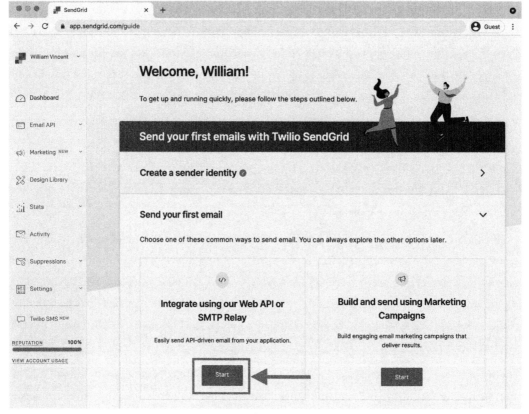

SendGrid welcome screen

Now we have one more choice to make: Web API or SMTP Relay. We'll use SMTP *Relay* since it is the simpler choice and works well for our basic needs here. In a large-scale website you likely would want to use the Web API instead. Click on the "Choose" button under "SMTP Relay" to proceed.

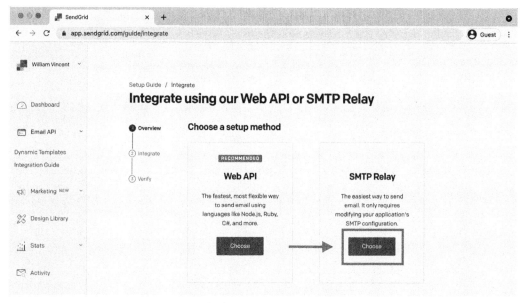

SendGrid Web API vs SMTP Relay

Ok, one more screen to navigate. Under step 1, "Create an API key," enter in a name for your first API Key. I've chosen the name "Newspaper" here. Then click on the blue "Create Key" button next to it.

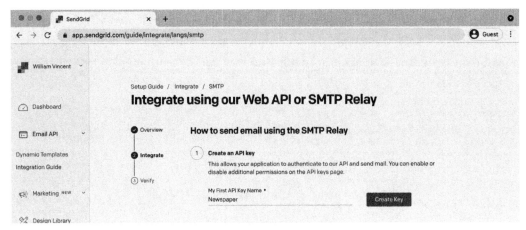

SendGrid integrate

The page will update and generate a custom API key in part 1 which is *also* our password in part 2. The username here, `apikey`, is the same for everyone but the password will be different for each account. Note that it matches our API key if we had wanted to go that route.

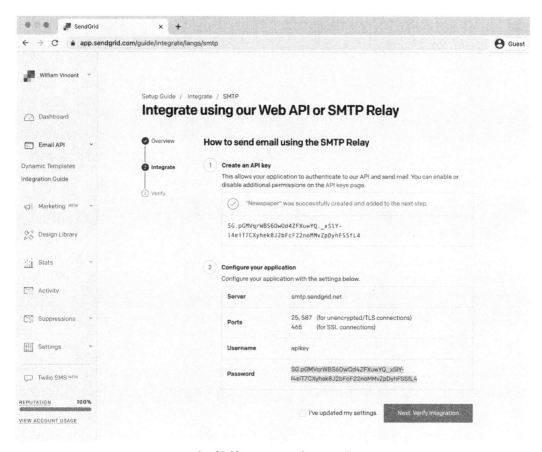

SendGrid username and password

Now it's time to add the new SendGrid username and password into our Django project. This won't take long!

First, in the `django_project/settings.py` file update the email backend to use SMTP. We already configured this once before near the bottom of the file. Instead of outputting emails to the console we want to instead send them for real using SMTP.

Code

```
# django_project/settings.py
EMAIL_BACKEND = "django.core.mail.backends.smtp.EmailBackend"  # new
```

Then, right below it, add the following six lines of email configuration. The DEFAULT_FROM_-
EMAIL[136] field is set, by default, to webmaster@localhost. You should update it with your intended
email account. Make sure to enter your own SendGrid EMAIL_HOST_PASSWORD here: sendgrid_-
password is just a placeholder!

Code

```
# django_project/settings.py
DEFAULT_FROM_EMAIL = "your_custom_email_account"
EMAIL_HOST = "smtp.sendgrid.net"
EMAIL_HOST_USER = "apikey"
EMAIL_HOST_PASSWORD = "sendgrid_password"
EMAIL_PORT = 587
EMAIL_USE_TLS = True
```

Note that an email password is information that should be kept secure and secret. Pasting it
in plain text into your codebase is a bad practice. And you definitely do *not* want to add it to
Git accidentally. In Chapter 16 we will learn how to add environment variables to our project so
that we can keep secret information truly secret. But for now, to keep things simple, we won't.
Technically we haven't added Git to our repo yet so we're ok but just be aware that any time
you are dealing with passwords or API keys alarm bells should be ringing in your ears around
security!

With that said, we're now complete and ready to confirm everything is working. The local server
should be already running at this point but if not, type python manage.py runserver to ensure
that it is.

Go *back* to the SendGrid "Integrate using our Web API or SMTP Relay" page and select the
checkbox next to "I've updated my settings." Then click on "Next: Verify Integration."

Navigate to the password reset form in your web browser, which should be located at:

```
http://127.0.0.1:8000/accounts/password_reset/
```

---

[136]https://docs.djangoproject.com/en/4.0/ref/settings/#default-from-email

Type in the email address for your superuser account which should be an email account you can access. *Do not* use the email for your SendGrid account; it should be different. Fill in the form and submit.

Now check your email inbox. You should see a new email there from your `DEFAULT_FROM_EMAIL` email address which was just verified. The text will be exactly the same as that outputted to our command line console previously.

The final step is to return to SendGrid and click on the blue button to "Verify Integration."

SendGrid verify integration

The button will turn grey and display "Checking..." for a moment until displaying "It worked!"

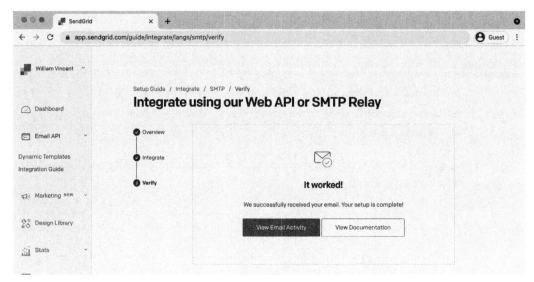

SendGrid it worked

Phew. We're done! That was a lot of steps but our real-world email integration is now working.

Custom Emails

The current email text isn't very personal, is it? Let's change things. At this point I could just show you what steps to take, but I think it's helpful to instead explain **how** I figured out how to do this. After all, you want to be able to customize all parts of Django as needed.

In this case, I knew what text Django was using by default but it wasn't clear where in the Django source code it was written. And since all of Django's source code is available on Github[137] we can can just search it.

Use the Github search bar and enter a few words from the email text. For example, "You're receiving this email because" and make sure to search "in this repository". There are a number of results that appear but the first result is the one we want. It shows the code is located in the `contrib` app in a file called `password_reset_email.html`.

---

[137]https://github.com/django/django

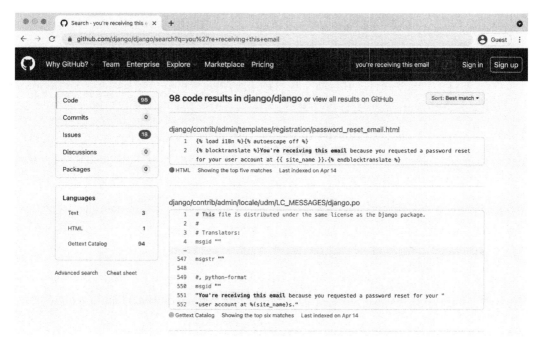

GitHub search result

The complete link for the file is quite long:

django/contrib/admin/templates/registration/password_reset_email.html

Here is that default text from the Django source code.

Code

```
{% load i18n %}{% autoescape off %}
{% blocktranslate %}You're receiving this email because you requested a password reset
for your user account at {{ site_name }}.{% endblocktranslate %}

{% translate "Please go to the following page and choose a new password:" %}
{% block reset_link %}
{{ protocol }}://{{ domain }}{% url 'password_reset_confirm' uidb64=uid token=token %}
{% endblock %}
{% translate "Your username, in case you've forgotten:" %} {{ user.get_username }}

{% translate "Thanks for using our site!" %}

{% blocktranslate %}The {{ site_name }} team{% endblocktranslate %}

{% endautoescape %}
```

To make changes create a new `templates/registration/password_reset_email.html` file in your own project. Then copy and paste the code from the Django repo into it. If you want to customize the text, you can.

This code might look a little scary so let's break it down line-by-line. Up top we load the template tag i18n[138] which means this text is eligible to be translated into multiple languages. Django has robust internationalization support[139] though covering it is beyond the scope of this book.

We're greeting the user by name thanks to `user.get_username`. Then we use the `reset_link` block to include the custom URL link. You can read more about Django's password management approach[140] in the official docs.

Let's also update the email's subject title. To do this we'll create another new file called `templates/registration/password_reset_subject.txt`. Add the following line of code to it:

Code

```
Please reset your password
```

And we're all set. Go ahead and try out our new flow again by entering a new password at `http://127.0.0.1:8000/accounts/password_reset/`. Then check your email and it will have the desired content and updated subject.

Conclusion

We've now finished implementing a complete user authentication flow. Users can sign up for a new account, log in, log out, change their password, and reset their password. We have learned how to customize all the templates involve and integrate with an email provider to actually send the emails. It's time to build out our actual *Newspaper* app.

---

[138] https://docs.djangoproject.com/en/4.0/ref/templates/builtins/#i18n
[139] https://docs.djangoproject.com/en/4.0/topics/i18n/
[140] https://docs.djangoproject.com/en/4.0/topics/auth/passwords/

Chapter 13: Newspaper App

It's time to build out our *Newspaper* app. We will have an articles page where journalists can post articles, set up permissions so only the author of an article can edit or delete it, and finally add the ability for other users to write comments on each article which will introduce the concept of foreign keys.

Articles App

To start create an `articles` app and define the database models. There are no hard and fast rules around what to name your apps except that you can't use the name of a built-in app. If you look at the `INSTALLED_APPS` section of `django_project/settings.py` you can see which app names are off-limits:

- `admin`
- `auth`
- `contenttypes`
- `sessions`
- `messages`
- `staticfiles`.

A general rule of thumb is to use the plural of an app name–`posts`, `payments`, `users`, etc.–unless doing so is obviously wrong as in the common case of `blog` where the singular makes more sense.

Start by creating our new `articles` app.

Shell

```
(.venv) > python manage.py startapp articles
```

Then add it to our INSTALLED_APPS and update the time zone since we'll be timestamping our articles. You can find your time zone in this Wikipedia list[141]. For example, I live in Boston, MA which is in the Eastern time zone of the United States. Therefore my entry is America/New_York.

Code

```
# django_project/settings.py
INSTALLED_APPS = [
    "django.contrib.admin",
    "django.contrib.auth",
    "django.contrib.contenttypes",
    "django.contrib.sessions",
    "django.contrib.messages",
    "django.contrib.staticfiles",
    # 3rd Party
    "crispy_forms",
    "crispy_bootstrap5",
    # Local
    "accounts.apps.AccountsConfig",
    "pages.apps.PagesConfig",
    "articles.apps.ArticlesConfig",  # new
]

TIME_ZONE = "America/New_York"  # new
```

Next up we define our database model which contains four fields: title, body, date, and author. Note that we're letting Django automatically set the time and date based on our TIME_ZONE setting. For the author field we want to reference our custom user model[142] "accounts.CustomUser" which we set in the django_project/settings.py file as AUTH_USER_MODEL. We will also implement the best practice of defining a get_absolute_url and a __str__ method for viewing the model in our admin interface.

---

[141]https://en.wikipedia.org/wiki/List_of_tz_database_time_zones
[142]https://docs.djangoproject.com/en/4.0/topics/auth/customizing/#django.contrib.auth.get_user_model

Code

```python
# articles/models.py
from django.conf import settings
from django.db import models
from django.urls import reverse


class Article(models.Model):
    title = models.CharField(max_length=255)
    body = models.TextField()
    date = models.DateTimeField(auto_now_add=True)
    author = models.ForeignKey(
        settings.AUTH_USER_MODEL,
        on_delete=models.CASCADE,
    )

    def __str__(self):
        return self.title

    def get_absolute_url(self):
        return reverse("article_detail", kwargs={"pk": self.pk})
```

Note that there are two main ways to refer to a custom user model: AUTH_USER_MODEL and get_-
user_model[143]. As general advice:

- AUTH_USER_MODEL makes sense for references within a models.py file
- get_user_model() is recommended everywhere else such as views, tests, etc.

Since we have a brand new app and model, it's time to make a new migration file and then apply
it to the database.

Shell

```
(.venv) > python manage.py makemigrations articles
(.venv) > python manage.py migrate
```

At this point I like to jump into the admin to play around with the model before building out the
urls/views/templates needed to actually display the data on the website. But first we need to
update articles/admin.py so our new app is displayed.

---

[143]https://docs.djangoproject.com/en/4.0/topics/auth/customizing/#django.contrib.auth.get_user_model

Code

```
# articles/admin.py
from django.contrib import admin
from .models import Article

admin.site.register(Article)
```

Now we start the server.

Shell

```
(.venv) > python manage.py runserver
```

And navigate to the admin at `http://127.0.0.1:8000/admin/` and log in.

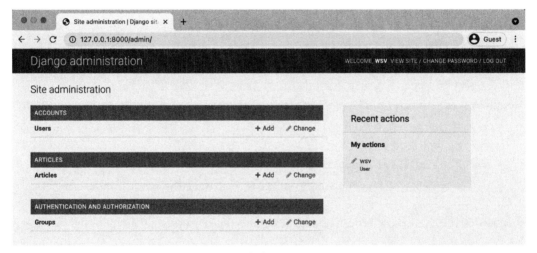

Admin page

If you click on "+ Add" next to "Articles" at the top of the page we can enter in some sample data. You'll likely have three users available at this point: your `superuser`, `testuser`, and `testuser2` accounts. Use your superuser account as the `author` of all three articles. I've added three new articles as you can see on the updated Articles page.

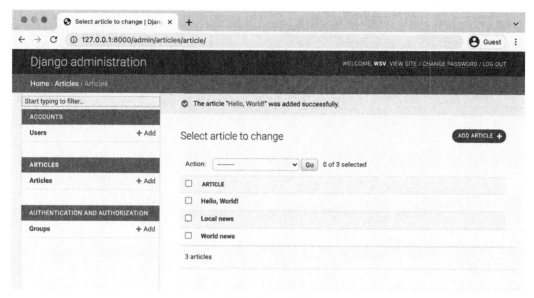

Admin three articles

If you click on an individual article you will see that the `title`, `body`, and `author` are displayed but not the `date`. That's because the `date` was automatically added by Django for us and therefore can't be changed in the admin. We *could* make the date editable–in more complex apps it's common to have both a `created_at` and `updated_at` field–but to keep things simple we'll just have the `date` be set upon creation by Django for us for now. Even though `date` is not displayed here we will still be able to access it in our templates so it can be displayed on web pages.

URLs and Views

The next step is to configure our URLs and views. Let's have our articles appear at `articles/`. Add a URL pattern for `articles` in our `django_project/urls.py` file.

Code

```
# django_project/urls.py
from django.contrib import admin
from django.urls import path, include

urlpatterns = [
    path("admin/", admin.site.urls),
    path("accounts/", include("accounts.urls")),
    path("accounts/", include("django.contrib.auth.urls")),
    path("articles/", include("articles.urls")),  # new
    path("", include("pages.urls")),
]
```

Next we create a new `articles/urls.py` file in the text editor and populate it with our routes. Let's start with the page to list all articles at `articles/` which will use the view `ArticleListView`.

Code

```
# articles/urls.py
from django.urls import path

from .views import ArticleListView

urlpatterns = [
    path("", ArticleListView.as_view(), name="article_list"),
]
```

Now create our view using the built-in generic `ListView` from Django. The only two fields we need to specify are the model `Article` and our template name which will be `article_list.html`.

Code

```
# articles/views.py
from django.views.generic import ListView

from .models import Article


class ArticleListView(ListView):
    model = Article
    template_name = "article_list.html"
```

The last step is to create a new template file in the text editor called `templates/article_-list.html`. Bootstrap has a built-in component called Cards[144] that we can customize for our individual articles. Recall that `ListView` returns an object with `<model_name>_list` that we can iterate over using a `for` loop.

Within each `article` we display the title, body, author, and date. We can even provide links to "edit" and "delete" functionality that we haven't built yet.

Code

```
<!-- templates/article_list.html -->
{% extends "base.html" %}

{% block title %}Articles{% endblock title %}

{% block content %}
{% for article in article_list %}
  <div class="card">
    <div class="card-header">
      <span class="font-weight-bold">{{ article.title }}</span> &middot;
      <span class="text-muted">by {{ article.author }} |
      {{ article.date }}</span>
    </div>
    <div class="card-body">
      {{ article.body }}
    </div>
    <div class="card-footer text-center text-muted">
      <a href="#">Edit</a> | <a href="#">Delete</a>
    </div>
```

---

[144]https://getbootstrap.com/docs/5.1/components/card/

```
    </div>
    <br />
{% endfor %}
{% endblock content %}
```

Spin up the server again with `python manage.py runserver` and check out our page at `http://127.0.0.1:8000/articles/`.

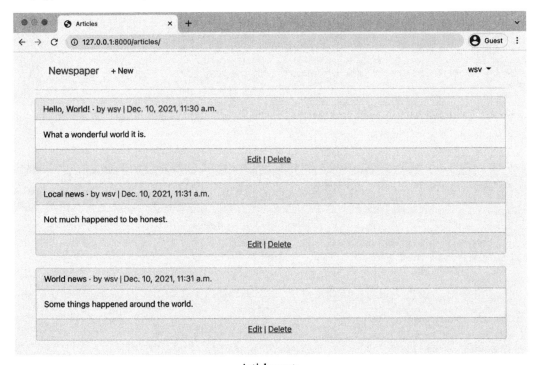

Articles page

Not bad eh? If we wanted to get fancy we could create a custom template filter[145] so that the date outputted is shown in seconds, minutes, or days. This can be done with some if/else logic and Django's date options[146] but we won't implement it here.

---

[145]https://docs.djangoproject.com/en/4.0/howto/custom-template-tags/
[146]https://docs.djangoproject.com/en/4.0/ref/templates/builtins/#date

Detail/Edit/Delete

The next step is to add detail, edit, and delete options for the articles. That means new urls, views, and templates. Let's start with the URLs. The Django ORM automatically adds a primary key to each database entry, meaning that the first article has a pk value of 1, the second of 2, and so on. We can use this to craft our URL paths.

For our detail page we want the route to be at articles/<int:pk>. The int here is known as a path converter[147] and essentially tells Django we want this value to be treated as an integer and not another data type like a string. Therefore the URL route for the first article will be at <articles/1/. Since we are in the articles app all URL routes will be prefixed with articles because we set that in django_project/urls.py. We only need to add the <int:pk> part here.

Next up are the edit and delete routes. They will also use the primary key and be at articles/1/edit/ and articles/1/delete/ as the eventual routes. Here is how the updated articles/urls.py file should look.

Code

```
# articles/urls.py
from django.urls import path

from .views import (
    ArticleListView,
    ArticleDetailView,   # new
    ArticleUpdateView,   # new
    ArticleDeleteView,   # new
)

urlpatterns = [
    path("<int:pk>/", ArticleDetailView.as_view(),
        name="article_detail"),   # new
    path("<int:pk>/edit/", ArticleUpdateView.as_view(),
        name="article_edit"),   # new
    path("<int:pk>/delete/", ArticleDeleteView.as_view(),
        name="article_delete"),   # new
    path("", ArticleListView.as_view(),
        name="article_list"),
]
```

[147]https://docs.djangoproject.com/en/4.0/topics/http/urls/#path-converters

For our views we will use Django's generic class-based views for `DetailView`, `UpdateView` and `DeleteView`. The detail view only requires listing the model and template name. For the update/edit view we also add the specific fields–`title` and `body`–that can be changed. And for the delete view we must add a redirect for where to send the user after deleting the entry. That requires importing `reverse_lazy` and specifying the `success_url` along with a corresponding named URL.

Code

```
# articles/views.py
from django.views.generic import ListView, DetailView  # new
from django.views.generic.edit import UpdateView, DeleteView   # new
from django.urls import reverse_lazy  # new
from .models import Article


class ArticleListView(ListView):
    model = Article
    template_name = "article_list.html"


class ArticleDetailView(DetailView):  # new
    model = Article
    template_name = "article_detail.html"


class ArticleUpdateView(UpdateView):  # new
    model = Article
    fields = (
        "title",
        "body",
    )
    template_name = "article_edit.html"


class ArticleDeleteView(DeleteView):  # new
    model = Article
    template_name = "article_delete.html"
    success_url = reverse_lazy("article_list")
```

If you recall the acronym CRUD (*Create-Read-Update-Delete*) from Chapter 6 you'll see that we are implementing three of the four functionalities here. We'll add the fourth, for create, later on in this chapter. Almost every website uses CRUD and this pattern will quickly feel quite natural when using Django or any other web framework.

The URL paths and views are done so the final step is to add templates. Create three new template files in your text editor:

- `templates/article_detail.html`
- `templates/article_edit.html`
- `templates/article_delete.html`

We'll start with the details page which will display the title, date, body, and author with links to edit and delete. It will also link back to all articles. Recall that the Django templating language's `url` tag wants the URL name and then any arguments passed in. The name of our edit route is `article_edit` and we need to pass in its primary key `article.pk`. The delete route name is `article_delete` and it also needs a primary key `article.pk`. Our `articles` page is a `ListView` so it does not need any additional arguments passed in.

Code

```
<!-- templates/article_detail.html -->
{% extends "base.html" %}

{% block content %}
<div class="article-entry">
  <h2>{{ object.title }}</h2>
  <p>by {{ object.author }} | {{ object.date }}</p>
  <p>{{ object.body }}</p>
</div>

<p><a href="{% url 'article_edit' article.pk %}">Edit</a> |
  <a href="{% url 'article_delete' article.pk %}">Delete</a></p>
<p>Back to <a href="{% url 'article_list' %}">All Articles</a>.</p>
{% endblock content %}
```

For the edit and delete pages we can use Bootstrap's button styling[148] to make the edit button light blue and the delete button red.

---

[148] https://getbootstrap.com/docs/5.1/components/buttons/

Code

```
<!-- templates/article_edit.html -->
{% extends "base.html" %}
{% load crispy_forms_tags %}

{% block content %}
<h1>Edit</h1>
<form action="" method="post">{% csrf_token %}
  {{ form|crispy }}
  <button class="btn btn-info ml-2" type="submit">Update</button>
</form>
{% endblock content %}
```

Code

```
<!-- templates/article_delete.html -->
{% extends "base.html" %}

{% block content %}
<h1>Delete</h1>
<form action="" method="post">{% csrf_token %}
  <p>Are you sure you want to delete "{{ article.title }}"?</p>
  <button class="btn btn-danger ml-2" type="submit">Confirm</button>
</form>
{% endblock content %}
```

As a final step, in the `card-footer` section of `article_list.html` we can add our URL routes to the current `a href` placeholders by using the url[149] template tag, the URL name, and the `pk` of each article.

---

[149]https://docs.djangoproject.com/en/4.0/ref/templates/builtins/#url

Code

```
<!-- templates/article_list.html -->
...
<div class="card-footer text-center text-muted">
  <a href="{% url 'article_edit' article.pk %}">Edit</a> |
  <a href="{% url 'article_delete' article.pk %}">Delete</a>
</div>
...
```

Ok, we're ready to view our work. Start up the server with `python manage.py runserver` and navigate to articles page at `http://127.0.0.1:8000/articles/`. Click the "edit" link next to the first article and you'll be redirected to `http://127.0.0.1:8000/articles/1/edit/`.

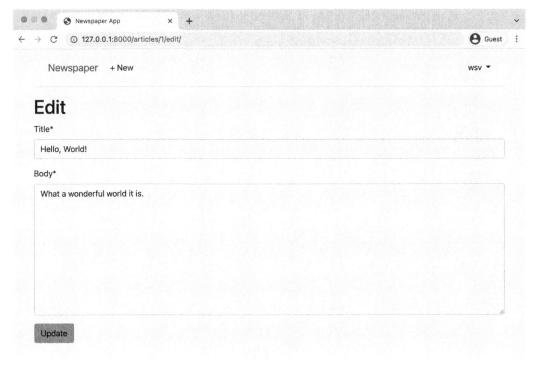

Edit page

If you update the "title" field by adding "(edited)" at the end and click "Update" you'll be redirected to the detail page which shows the new change.

Detail page

If you click on the "Delete" link you'll be redirected to the delete page.

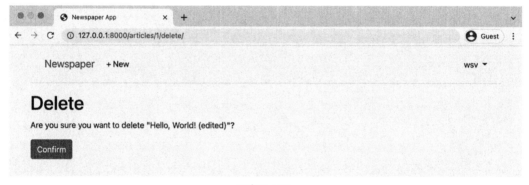

Delete page

Press the scary red button for "Confirm" and you'll be redirected to the articles page which now only has two entries.

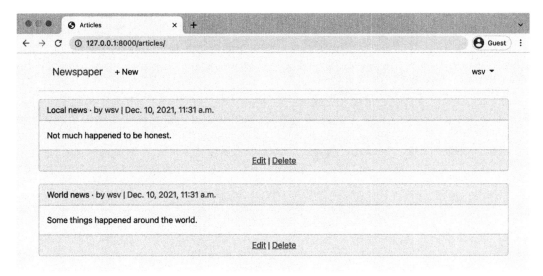

Articles page two entries

Create Page

The final step is a create page for new articles which we can implement with Django's built-in `CreateView`. Our three steps are to create a view, url, and template. This flow should feel pretty familiar by now.

In the `articles/views.py` file add `CreateView` to the imports at the top and make a new class at the bottom of the file called `ArticleCreateView` that specifies our model, template, and the fields available.

Code

```
# articles/views.py
...
from django.views.generic.edit import (
    UpdateView, DeleteView, CreateView # new
)
...
class ArticleCreateView(CreateView):  # new
    model = Article
    template_name = "article_new.html"
    fields = (
        "title",
        "body",
        "author",
    )
```

Note that our fields has author since we want to associate a new article with an author, however once an article has been created we do not want a user to be able to change the author which is why ArticleUpdateView only has the fields ['title', 'body',].

Now update the articles/urls.py file with the new route for the view.

Code

```
# articles/urls.py
from django.urls import path

from .views import (
    ArticleListView,
    ArticleDetailView,
    ArticleUpdateView,
    ArticleDeleteView,
    ArticleCreateView, # new
)

urlpatterns = [
    path("<int:pk>/",
        ArticleDetailView.as_view(), name="article_detail"),
    path("<int:pk>/edit/",
        ArticleUpdateView.as_view(), name="article_edit"),
    path("<int:pk>/delete/",
        ArticleDeleteView.as_view(), name="article_delete"),
    path("new/", ArticleCreateView.as_view(), name="article_new"),  # new
```

```
    path("", ArticleListView.as_view(), name="article_list"),
]
```

To complete the new create functionality add a new template named `templates/article_-new.html` and update it with the following HTML code.

Code

```
<!-- templates/article_new.html -->
{% extends "base.html" %}
{% load crispy_forms_tags %}

{% block content %}
<h1>New article</h1>
<form action="" method="post">{% csrf_token %}
  {{ form|crispy }}
  <button class="btn btn-success ml-2" type="submit">Save</button>
</form>
{% endblock content %}
```

Finally, we should add the URL link for creating new articles to our navbar so it is accessible everywhere on the site to logged-in users.

Code

```
<!-- templates/base.html -->
...
{% if user.is_authenticated %}
  <li><a href="{% url 'article_new' %}"
    class="nav-link px-2 link-dark">+ New</a></li>
...
```

If you need help to make sure your HTML file is accurate now, please refer to the official source code[150].

We're all done. Let's just confirm everything works as expected. Click on "Newspaper" link in the top navbar which directs users to the homepage. Then click on the link for "+ New" in the top navbar and you'll be redirected to our create page.

---

[150]https://github.com/wsvincent/djangoforbeginners/blob/master/ch13-newspaper-app/templates/base.html

Create page

Go ahead and create a new article. Then click on the "Save" button. You will be redirected to the detail page. Why? Because in our `models.py` file we set the `get_absolute_url` method to `article_detail`. This is a good approach because if we later change the url pattern for the detail page to, say, `articles/details/4/`, the redirect will still work. Whatever route is associated with `article_detail` will be used. There is no hardcoding of the route itself.

Detail page

Note also that the primary key here is 4 in the URL. Even though we're only displaying three articles right now, Django doesn't reorder the primary keys just because we deleted one. In practice, most real-world sites don't actually delete anything; instead they "hide" deleted fields since this makes it easier to maintain the integrity of a database and gives the option to "undelete" later on if needed. With our current approach though once something is deleted it's gone for good!

Click on the link for "All Articles" to see our new /articles page.

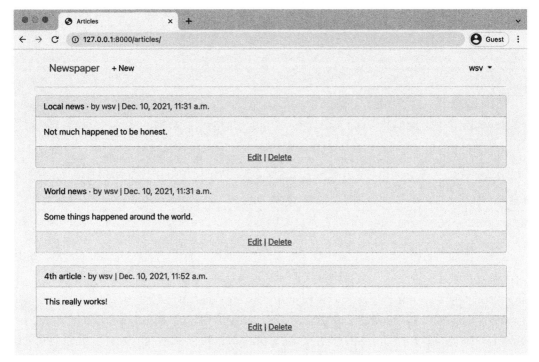

Updated articles page

There's our new article entry on the bottom as expected.

Conclusion

We have created a dedicated `articles` app with CRUD functionality. Articles can be created, read, updated, deleted, and even viewed as an entire list. But there are no permissions or authorizations yet, which means anyone can do anything! If a logged-out user knows the correct URLs they can make edits or deletes to an existing article, even one that's not their own! In the next chapter we will add permissions and authorizations to our project to fix this.

Chapter 14: Permissions and Authorization

There are several issues with our current *Newspaper* website. For one thing we want our newspaper to be financially sustainable. With more time we could add a dedicated `payments` app to charge for access, but for now we will require a user to log in to view any articles. This is known as *authorization*. It's common to set different rules around who is authorized to view areas of your site. Note that this is different than **authentication** which is the process of registering and logging-in users. Authorization restricts access; authentication enables a user sign up and log in flow.

As a mature web framework, Django has built-in functionality for authorization that we can quickly use. In this chapter we'll limit access to the articles list page to only logged-in users and add additional restrictions so that only the author of an article can edit or delete it.

Improved CreateView

At present the `author` on a new article can be set to any existing user. Instead it should be automatically set to the current logged-in user. We can modify Django's `CreateView` to achieve this by removing `author` from the `fields` and setting it automatically via the `form_valid` method instead.

Code

```
# articles/views.py
class ArticleCreateView(CreateView):
    model = Article
    template_name = "article_new.html"
    fields = ("title", "body")  # new

    def form_valid(self, form):  # new
        form.instance.author = self.request.user
        return super().form_valid(form)
```

How did I know I could update `CreateView` like this? The answer is I looked at the source code and used Classy Class-Based Views[151], an amazing resource that breaks down how each generic class-based view actually works in Django. Generic class-based views are great but when you want to customize them it is necessary roll up your sleeves and start to understand what's actually going on under the hood. This is the downside of class-based views vs function-based views: more is hidden and the inheritance chain must be understood. The more you use and customize built-in views, the more comfortable you will become making customizations like this. Generally there is a specific method, like `form_valid`, that can be overridden to achieve your desired result instead of having to re-write everything from scratch yourself.

Now reload the browser and try clicking on the "+ New" link in the top nav. It will redirect to the updated create page where `author` is no longer a field.

---

[151]https://ccbv.co.uk/

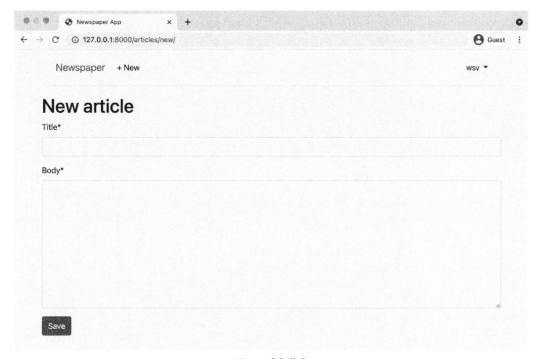

New article link

If you create a new article and then go into the admin you will see it is automatically set to the current logged-in user.

Authorizations

There are multiple issues around the lack of authorizations in our current project. Obviously we would like to restrict access to only users so we have the option of one day charging readers to our newspaper. But beyond that, any random logged-out user who knows the correct URL can access any part of the site.

Consider what would happen if a logged-out user tried to create a new article? To try it out, click on your username in the upper right corner of the nav bar, then select "Log Out" from the dropdown options. The "+ New" link disappears from the nav bar but what happens if you go to it directly: `http://127.0.0.1:8000/articles/new/`?

The page is still there.

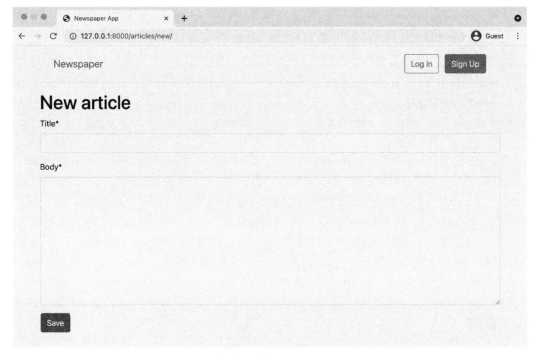

Logged out new

Now try to create a new article with a title and body. Click on the "Save" button.

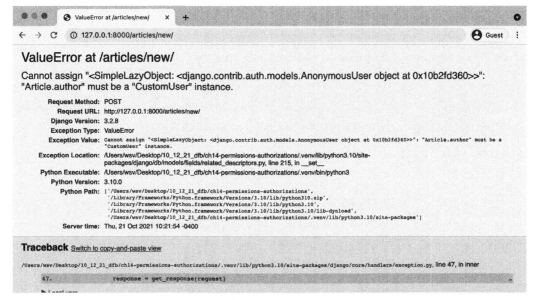

Create page error

An error! This is because our model **expects** an author field which is linked to the current logged-in user. But since we are not logged in, there's no author, and therefore the submission fails. What to do?

Mixins

We clearly want to set some authorizations so only logged-in users can access certain URLs. To do this we can use a *mixin*, which is a special kind of multiple inheritance that Django uses to avoid duplicate code and still allow customization. For example, the built-in generic ListView[152] needs a way to return a template. But so does DetailView[153] and in fact almost every other view. Rather than repeat the same code in each big generic view, Django breaks out this functionality into a mixin known as TemplateResponseMixin[154]. Both `ListView` and `DetailView` use this mixin to render the proper template.

---

[152]https://docs.djangoproject.com/en/4.0/ref/class-based-views/generic-display/#django.views.generic.list.ListView

[153]https://docs.djangoproject.com/en/4.0/ref/class-based-views/generic-display/#detailview

[154]https://docs.djangoproject.com/en/4.0/ref/class-based-views/mixins-simple/#templateresponsemixin

If you read the Django source code, which is freely available on Github[155], you'll see mixins used all over the place. To restrict view access to only logged in users, Django has a LoginRequired mixin[156] that we can use. It's powerful and extremely concise.

In the `articles/views.py` file, import `LoginRequiredMixin` at the top and then it add to the `ArticleCreateView`. Make sure that the mixin is to the left of `CreateView` so it will be read first. We want the `CreateView` to already know we intend to restrict access.

And that's it! We're done.

Code

```
# articles/views.py
from django.contrib.auth.mixins import LoginRequiredMixin  # new
from django.views.generic import ListView, DetailView
...


class ArticleCreateView(LoginRequiredMixin, CreateView):  # new
    ...
```

Now return to the homepage at `http://127.0.0.1:8000/` to avoid resubmitting the form. Navigate to `http://127.0.0.1:8000/articles/new/` again to access the URL route for a new article.

---

[155]https://github.com/django/django
[156]https://docs.djangoproject.com/en/4.0/topics/auth/default/#the-loginrequired-mixin

Log In Redirect Page

What's happening? Django automatically redirected users to the log in page! If you look closely, the URL is `http://127.0.0.1:8000/accounts/login/?next=/articles/new/` which shows we *tried* to go to `articles/new/` but were instead redirected to log in.

LoginRequiredMixin

Restricting view access requires adding `LoginRequiredMixin` at the beginning of all existing views. Let's update the rest of our `articles` views since we don't want a user to be able to create, read, update, or delete a message if they aren't logged in.

The complete `views.py` file should now look like this:

Code

```python
# articles/views.py
from django.contrib.auth.mixins import LoginRequiredMixin
from django.views.generic import ListView, DetailView
from django.views.generic.edit import CreateView, UpdateView, DeleteView
from django.urls import reverse_lazy

from .models import Article


class ArticleListView(LoginRequiredMixin, ListView):  # new
    model = Article
    template_name = "article_list.html"


class ArticleDetailView(LoginRequiredMixin, DetailView):  # new
    model = Article
    template_name = "article_detail.html"


class ArticleUpdateView(LoginRequiredMixin, UpdateView):  # new
    model = Article
    fields = (
        "title",
        "body",
    )
    template_name = "article_edit.html"


class ArticleDeleteView(LoginRequiredMixin, DeleteView):  # new
    model = Article
    template_name = "article_delete.html"
    success_url = reverse_lazy("article_list")


class ArticleCreateView(LoginRequiredMixin, CreateView):
    model = Article
    template_name = "article_new.html"
    fields = ("title", "body",)

    def form_valid(self, form):
        form.instance.author = self.request.user
        return super().form_valid(form)
```

Go ahead and play around with the site to confirm that the log in redirects now work as expected. If you need help recalling what the proper URLs are, log in first and write down the URLs for each of the routes for create, edit, delete, and list all articles.

UpdateView and DeleteView

We're making progress but there's still the issue of our edit and delete views. Any *logged in* user can make changes to any article. What we want is to restrict this access so that only the author of an article has this permission.

We could add permissions logic to each view for this but a more elegant solution is to create a dedicated mixin, a class with a particular feature that we want to reuse in our Django code. And better yet, Django ships with a built-in mixin, UserPassesTestMixin[157], just for this purpose!

To use UserPassesTestMixin, first import it at the top of the articles/views.py file and then add it to both the update and delete views where we want this restriction. The test_func method is used by UserPassesTestMixin for our logic. We need to override it. In this case we set the variable obj to the current object returned by the view using get_object(). Then we say, if the author on the current object matches the current user on the webpage (whoever is logged in and trying to make the change), then allow it. If false, an error will automatically be thrown.

The code looks like this:

---

[157]https://docs.djangoproject.com/en/4.0/topics/auth/default/#django.contrib.auth.mixins. UserPassesTestMixin

Code

```
# articles/views.py
from django.contrib.auth.mixins import (
    LoginRequiredMixin,
    UserPassesTestMixin # new
)
from django.views.generic import ListView, DetailView
from django.views.generic.edit import UpdateView, DeleteView, CreateView
from django.urls import reverse_lazy

from .models import Article
...
class ArticleUpdateView(
  LoginRequiredMixin, UserPassesTestMixin, UpdateView):  # new
    model = Article
    fields = (
        "title",
        "body",
    )
    template_name = "article_edit.html"

    def test_func(self):  # new
        obj = self.get_object()
        return obj.author == self.request.user


class ArticleDeleteView(
  LoginRequiredMixin, UserPassesTestMixin, DeleteView):  # new
    model = Article
    template_name = "article_delete.html"
    success_url = reverse_lazy("article_list")

    def test_func(self):  # new
        obj = self.get_object()
        return obj.author == self.request.user
```

When using mixins with class-based views the order is very important. `LoginRequiredMixin` comes first so that we force log in, then we add `UserPassesTestMixin` for an additional layer of functionality on top of it, and finally either `UpdateView` or `DeleteView`. If you do not have this order in place the code will not work properly.

Log in with your `testuser` account and go to the articles list page. If the code works, then you should not be able to edit or delete any posts written by your superuser, which is all of them right now. Instead you will see a Permission Denied 403 error page.

403 error page

However if you create a new article with `testuser` you *will* be able to edit or delete it. And if you log in with your `superuser` account instead, you can edit or delete posts written by that author.

Conclusion

Our *Newspaper* app is almost done. There are further steps we could take at this point, such as only displaying edit and delete links to the appropriate users, which would involve custom template tags[158] but overall the app is in good shape. We have our articles properly configured, set permissions and authorizations, and set up our user authentication flow. The last item needed is the ability for fellow logged-in users to leave comments which we'll cover in the next chapter.

---

[158]https://docs.djangoproject.com/en/4.0/howto/custom-template-tags/

Chapter 15: Comments

There are two ways we could add comments to our *Newspaper* site. The first is to create a dedicated *comments* app and link it to *articles*, however that seems like over-engineering at this point. Instead, we can simply add an additional model called `Comment` to our *articles* app and link it to the `Article` model through a foreign key. We will take the simpler approach since it's always easy to add more complexity later.

The whole structure within Django of one project and multiple smaller apps is designed to help the developer reason about the website. The computer doesn't care how the code is structured. Breaking functionality out into smaller pieces helps us–and any future teammates–understand the logic in a web application. But you don't need to prematurely optimize. If your eventual comments logic becomes quite lengthy then yes, by all means, spin it off into its own `comments` app. But the first thing to do is make the code work, then make sure it is performant, and lastly structure it so it's understandable to you or someone else months later.

What do we need to add comments functionality to our website? We already know it will involve models, urls, views, templates, and in this case also forms. All will be needed for the final solution but the order in which we tackle them is largely up to us. That said, many Django developers find that going in this order–models -> urls -> views -> templates/forms–works best so that is what we will use here. By the end of this chapter, users will be able to add comments to any existing article on our website.

Model

Let's begin by adding another table to our existing database called `Comment`. This model will have a many-to-one foreign key relationship to `Article`: one article can have many comments, but not the other way around. Traditionally the name of the foreign key field is simply the model it links to, so this field will be called `article`. The other two fields will be `comment` and `author`.

Open up the file `articles/models.py` and underneath the existing code add the following. Note that we are including both a `__str__` and `get_absolute_url` method as a best practice.

Code

```
# articles/models.py
...
class Comment(models.Model):  # new
    article = models.ForeignKey(Article, on_delete=models.CASCADE)
    comment = models.CharField(max_length=140)
    author = models.ForeignKey(
        settings.AUTH_USER_MODEL,
        on_delete=models.CASCADE,
    )

    def __str__(self):
        return self.comment

    def get_absolute_url(self):
        return reverse("article_list")
```

Since we've updated our models it's time to make a new migration file and then apply it. Note that by adding `articles` at the end of the `makemigrations` command–which is optional–we are specifying we want to use just the `articles` app here. This is a good habit to use. For example, what if we made changes to models in two different apps? If we **did not** specify an app, then both apps's changes would be incorporated in the same migrations file which makes it harder, in the future, to debug errors. Keep each migration as small and contained as possible.

Shell

```
(.venv) > python manage.py makemigrations articles
(.venv) > python manage.py migrate
```

Admin

After making a new model it's good to play around with it in the admin app before displaying it on our actual website. Add `Comment` to our `admin.py` file so it will be visible.

Code

```
# articles/admin.py
from django.contrib import admin
from .models import Article, Comment  # new

admin.site.register(Article)
admin.site.register(Comment)  # new
```

Then start up the server with `python manage.py runserver` and navigate to our main page `http://127.0.0.1:8000/admin/`.

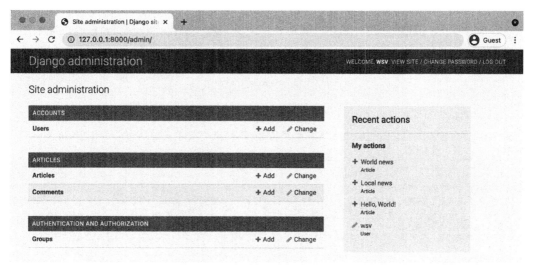

Admin page with comments

Under our app "Articles" you'll see our two tables: Comments and Articles. Click on the "+ Add" next to Comments. There are dropdowns for Article, Author, and a text field next to Comment.

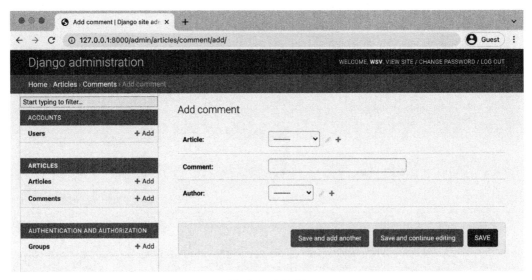

Admin comments

Select an Article, write a comment, and then choose an author that is not your superuser, perhaps `testuser` as I've done in the picture. Then click on the "Save" button.

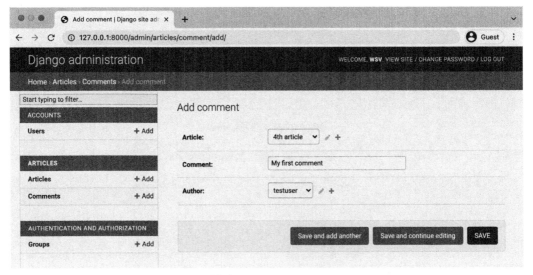

Admin testuser comment

You should next see your comment on the "Comments" page.

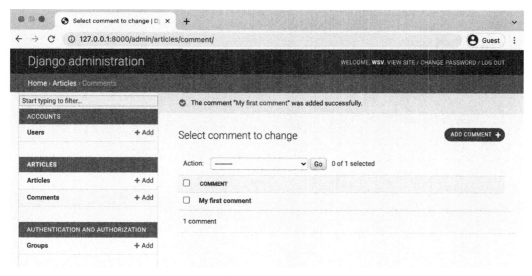

Admin comment one

At this point we could add an additional admin field so we'd see the comment and the article on this page. But wouldn't it be better to just see all `Comment` models related to a single `Article` model? It turns out we can with a Django admin feature called *inlines* which displays foreign key relationships in a visual way.

There are two main inline views used: TabularInline[159] and StackedInline[160]. The only difference between the two is the template for displaying information. In a TabularInline all model fields appear on one line while in a StackedInline each field has its own line. We'll implement both so you can decide which one you prefer.

Update `articles/admin.py` as follows in your text editor to add the StackedInline view.

[159]https://docs.djangoproject.com/en/4.0/ref/contrib/admin/#django.contrib.admin.TabularInline
[160]https://docs.djangoproject.com/en/4.0/ref/contrib/admin/#django.contrib.admin.StackedInline

Code

```
# articles/admin.py
from django.contrib import admin
from .models import Article, Comment


class CommentInline(admin.StackedInline):  # new
    model = Comment


class ArticleAdmin(admin.ModelAdmin):  # new
    inlines = [
        CommentInline,
    ]


admin.site.register(Article, ArticleAdmin)  # new
admin.site.register(Comment)
```

Now go back to the main admin page at `http://127.0.0.1:8000/admin/` and click on "Articles."
Select the article which you just added a comment for which was "4th article" in my case.

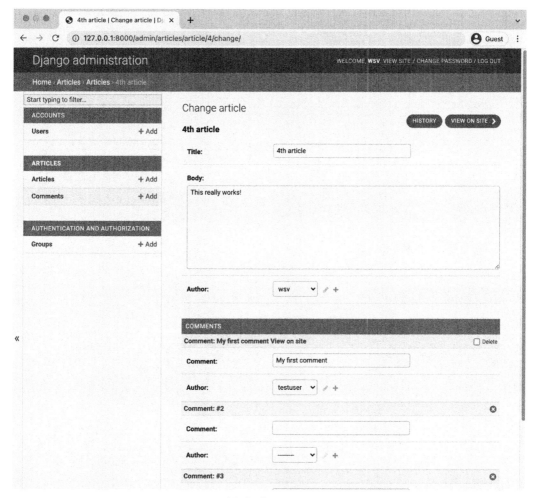

Admin change page

Better, right? We can see and modify all our related articles and comments in one place. Note that by default, the Django admin will display 3 empty rows here. You can change the default number that appear with the `extra` field. So if you wanted no extra fields by default, the code would look like this:

Code

```
# articles/admin.py
...
class CommentInline(admin.StackedInline):
    model = Comment
    extra = 0   # new
```

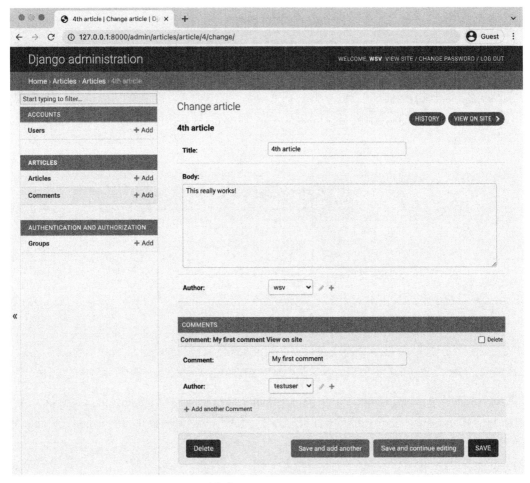

Admin no extra comments

Personally, though, I prefer using `TabularInline` as it shows more information in less space. To switch to it we only need to change our `CommentInline` from `admin.StackedInline` to `admin.TabularInline`.

Code

```
# articles/admin.py
from django.contrib import admin
from .models import Article, Comment


class CommentInline(admin.TabularInline):  # new
    model = Comment


class ArticleAdmin(admin.ModelAdmin):
    inlines = [
        CommentInline,
    ]


admin.site.register(Article, ArticleAdmin)
admin.site.register(Comment)
```

Refresh the current admin page for Articles and you'll see the new change: all fields for each model are displayed on the same line.

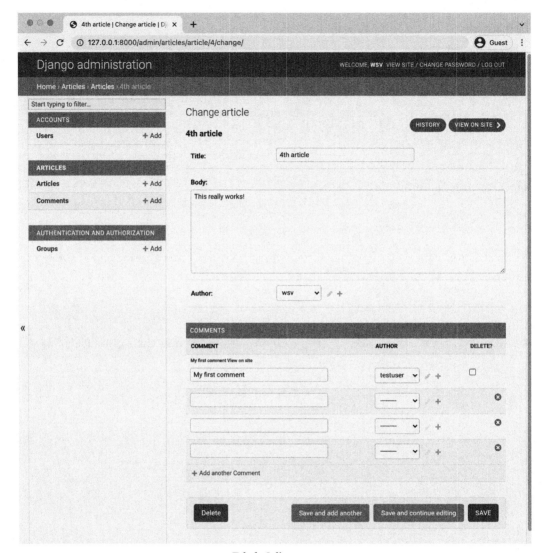

TabularInline page

Much better. Now we need to display the comments on our website by updating our template.

Template

We want comments to appear on the articles list page and allow logged-in users to add a comment on the detail page for an article. That means updating the template files `article_list.html` and `article_detail.html`.

Let's start with `article_list.html`. If you look at the `articles/models.py` file again it is clear that Comment has a foreign key relationship to Article. To display **all** comments related to a specific article we will follow the relationship backward[161] via a "query," which is a way to ask the database for a specific bit of information. Django has a built-in syntax for this known as `FOO_set` where `FOO` is the lowercased source model name. So for our `Article` model, in order to view all related comments, we use the syntax `{% for comment in article.comment_set.all %}`. And then within this `for` loop we can specify what to display such as the `comment` itself and `author`.

Here is what the updated `article_list.html` file looks like. The changes start after the `"card-body"` div class.

Code

```
<!-- templates/article_list.html -->
{% extends "base.html" %}

{% block title %}Articles{% endblock title %}

{% block content %}
{% for article in article_list %}
  <div class="card">
    <div class="card-header">
      <span class="font-weight-bold">{{ article.title }}</span> &middot;
      <span class="text-muted">by {{ article.author }} |
      {{ article.date }}</span>
    </div>
    <div class="card-body">
      <!-- Changes start here! -->
      <p>{{ article.body }}</p>
      <a href="{% url 'article_edit' article.pk %}">Edit</a> |
      <a href="{% url 'article_delete' article.pk %}">Delete</a>
    </div>
    <div class="card-footer">
```

---

[161]https://docs.djangoproject.com/en/4.0/topics/db/queries/#following-relationships-backward

```
    {% for comment in article.comment_set.all %}
      <p>
        <span class="font-weight-bold">
          {{ comment.author }} &middot;
        </span>
        {{ comment }}
      </p>
    {% endfor %}
  </div>
  <!-- Changes end here! -->
</div>
<br />
{% endfor %}
{% endblock content %}
```

If you refresh the articles page at http://127.0.0.1:8000/articles/ we can see our new comment displayed on the page.

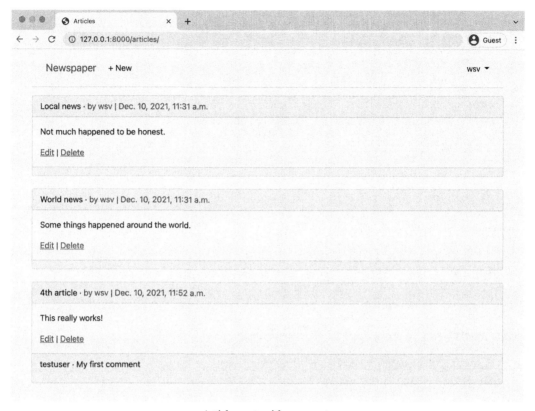

Articles page with comments

It works! We can see comments listed underneath the initial message. Let's also add comments to the detail page for each article. We'll use the exact same technique of following the relationship backwards to access comments as a foreign key of the article model.

Code

```
<!-- templates/article_detail.html -->
{% extends "base.html" %}

{% block content %}
<div class="article-entry">
  <h2>{{ object.title }}</h2>
  <p>by {{ object.author }} | {{ object.date }}</p>
  <p>{{ object.body }}</p>
</div>

<!-- Changes start here! -->
<hr>
<h4>Comments</h4>
{% for comment in article.comment_set.all %}
  <p>{{ comment.author }} &middot; {{ comment }}</p>
{% endfor %}
<hr>
<!-- Changes end here! -->

<p><a href="{% url 'article_edit' article.pk %}">Edit</a> |
  <a href="{% url 'article_delete' article.pk %}">Delete</a></p>
<p>Back to <a href="{% url 'article_list' %}">All Articles</a>.</p>
{% endblock content %}
```

Navigate to the detail page of your article with a comment and any comments will be visible.

Article details page with comments

We won't win any design awards for this layout but this is a book on Django so outputting the correct content is our goal.

Comment Form

The comments are now visible but we need to add a form so users can add them in the website itself. On the web forms are a very complicated topic since security is essential: any time you are accepting data from a user that will be stored in a database you must be extremely cautious. The good news is Django forms handle most of this work for us.

ModelForm[162] is a helper class designed to translate database models into forms. We can use it to create a form called, appropriately enough, `CommentForm`. We *could* put this form in our existing `articles/models.py` file but generally the best practice is to put all forms in a dedicated `forms.py` file within your app. That's the approach we'll use here.

With your text editor create a new file called `articles/forms.py`. At the top import `forms` which has `ModelForm` as a module. Then import our model, `Comment`, as well since we'll need to add that. And finally create the class `CommentForm` specifying both the underlying model and specific fields we wish to expose, which will be `comment` and `author`.

---

[162]https://docs.djangoproject.com/en/4.0/topics/forms/modelforms/#modelform

Code

```
# articles/forms.py
from django import forms

from .models import Comment


class CommentForm(forms.ModelForm):
    class Meta:
        model = Comment
        fields = ("comment", "author")
```

Web forms can be incredibly complex but Django has thankfully abstracted away much of the complexity for us.

Comment View

Currently we rely on the generic class-based `DetailView` to power our `ArticleDetailView`. It is well designed to display individual entries but it is not, by default, configured to add additional information like a form. Class-based views are powerful because their inheritance structure means that, if we know where to look, there is often a specific module we can override to attain our desired outcome.

The one we want in this case is called get_context_data()[163]. It is used to add information to a template by updating the context[164], a dictionary object containing all the variable names and values available in our template. For performance reasons Django templates are compiled only once so anything we want available in the template must be loaded from the beginning into the context.

What do we want to add in this case? Well, just our `CommentForm`. And since context is a dictionary we must assign a variable name as well. How about `form`? Here is what the new code looks like in `articles/views.py`.

---

[163]https://docs.djangoproject.com/en/4.0/ref/class-based-views/mixins-simple/#django.views.generic.base. ContextMixin.get_context_data

[164]https://docs.djangoproject.com/en/4.0/ref/templates/api/#django.template.Context

Code

```
# articles/views.py
from .forms import CommentForm  # new

class ArticleDetailView(LoginRequiredMixin, DetailView):
    model = Article
    template_name = "article_detail.html"

    def get_context_data(self, **kwargs):  # new
        context = super().get_context_data(**kwargs)
        context['form'] = CommentForm()
        return context
```

Near the top of the file we added an import line for `CommentForm` and then updated the module for `get_context_data()`. First we pulled all existing information into the context by using `super()`, then we added the variable name `form` with the value of `CommmentForm()`, and finally we returned the updated context.

Comment Template

To display the form in our `article_detail.html` template file we'll rely on the `form` variable and also crispy forms. This pattern is the same as what we've done before in our other forms. At the top load `crispy_form_tags`, create a standard-looking `post` form which uses a `csrf_token` for security, and display our form fields via `{{ form|crispy }}`.

Code

```
<!-- templates/article_detail.html -->
{% extends "base.html" %}
{% load crispy_forms_tags %} <!-- new! -->

{% block content %}
<div class="article-entry">
  <h2>{{ object.title }}</h2>
  <p>by {{ object.author }} | {{ object.date }}</p>
  <p>{{ object.body }}</p>
</div>

<hr>
```

```
<h4>Comments</h4>
{% for comment in article.comment_set.all %}
  <p>{{ comment.author }} &middot; {{ comment }}</p>
{% endfor %}
<hr>

<!-- Changes start here! -->
<h4>Add a comment</h4>
  <form action="" method="post">{% csrf_token %}
    {{ form|crispy }}
    <button class="btn btn-success ml-2" type="submit">Save</button>
  </form>
<!-- Changes end here! -->

<p><a href="{% url 'article_edit' article.pk %}">Edit</a> |
  <a href="{% url 'article_delete' article.pk %}">Delete</a></p>
<p>Back to <a href="{% url 'article_list' %}">All Articles</a>.</p>
{% endblock content %}
```

If you refresh the detail page the form is now displayed with familiar Bootstrap and crispy forms styling.

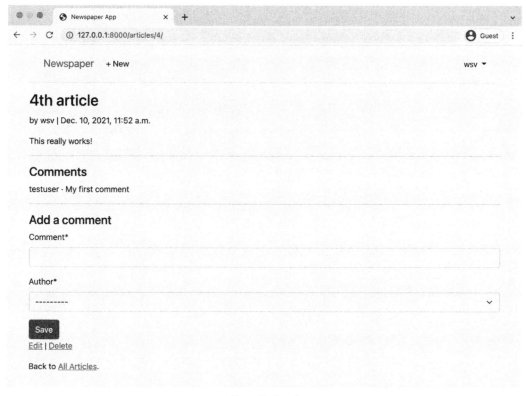

Form displayed

Success! However we are only half done. If you attempt to submit the form you'll receive an error because our view doesn't yet support any POST methods!

Comment Post View

What we ultimately need is a view that handles both GET and POST requests depending upon whether the form should be merely displayed or capable of being submitted. We could reach for FormMixin[165] to combine both into our ArticleDetailView but as the Django docs illustrate quite well[166], there are risks with this approach.

---

[165]https://docs.djangoproject.com/en/4.0/ref/class-based-views/mixins-editing/#django.views.generic.edit.FormMixin

[166]https://docs.djangoproject.com/en/4.0/topics/class-based-views/mixins/#avoid-anything-more-complex

To avoid subtle interactions between `DetailView` and `FormMixin` we will instead separate the `GET` and `POST` variations into their own dedicated views. We can then transform `ArticleDetailView` into a *wrapper view* that combines them. This is a very common pattern in more advanced Django development because it is often the case that a single URL must behave differently based on the user request (`GET`, `POST`, etc) or even the format (returning HTML vs JSON).

Let's start by renaming `ArticleDetailView` into `CommentGet` since it handles `GET` requests but not `POST` requests. We'll then create a new `CommentPost` view that is empty for now. And we can combine both into a new `ArticleDetailView` that subclasses View[167], the master class-based view upon which all the others classes are built.

Code

```
# articles/views.py
from django.views import View  # new


class CommentGet(DetailView):  # new
    model = Article
    template_name = "article_detail.html"

    def get_context_data(self, **kwargs):
        context = super().get_context_data(**kwargs)
        context["form"] = CommentForm()
        return context


class CommentPost():  # new
    pass


class ArticleDetailView(LoginRequiredMixin, View):  # new
    def get(self, request, *args, **kwargs):
        view = CommentGet.as_view()
        return view(request, *args, **kwargs)

    def post(self, request, *args, **kwargs):
        view = CommentPost.as_view()
        return view(request, *args, **kwargs)
```

---

[167]https://docs.djangoproject.com/en/4.0/ref/class-based-views/base/#django.views.generic.base.View

Navigate back to the homepage in your web browser and then reload the article page with a comment. Everything should work as before.

Ok, we're ready to write `CommentPost` and complete our task of adding comments to our website. Almost done!

FormView[168] is a built-in view that displays a form, any validation errors, and redirects to a new URL. We will use it in combination with SingleObjectMixin[169] which helps us associate the current article with our form. In other words, if you have a comment at `articles/4/`, as I do in the screenshots, this will grab the 4 so that our comment is saved to the article with a `pk` of 4.

Here is the complete new code which we'll run through line-by-line below.

Code

```
# articles/views.py
from django.contrib.auth.mixins import LoginRequiredMixin, UserPassesTestMixin
from django.views import View
from django.views.generic import ListView, DetailView, FormView  # new
from django.views.generic.detail import SingleObjectMixin  # new
from django.views.generic.edit import UpdateView, DeleteView, CreateView
from django.urls import reverse_lazy, reverse  # new

from .forms import CommentForm
from .models import Article

...
class CommentPost(SingleObjectMixin, FormView):  # new
    model = Article
    form_class = CommentForm
    template_name = "article_detail.html"

    def post(self, request, *args, **kwargs):
        self.object = self.get_object()
        return super().post(request, *args, **kwargs)

    def form_valid(self, form):
        comment = form.save(commit=False)
        comment.article = self.object
```

---

[168]https://docs.djangoproject.com/en/4.0/ref/class-based-views/generic-editing/#django.views.generic.edit.FormView

[169]https://docs.djangoproject.com/en/4.0/ref/class-based-views/mixins-single-object/#django.views.generic.detail.SingleObjectMixin

```
        comment.save()
        return super().form_valid(form)

    def get_success_url(self):
        article = self.get_object()
        return reverse("article_detail", kwargs={"pk": article.pk})
```

At the top import `FormView`, `SingleObjectMixin`, and `reverse`. FormView relies on `form_class` to
set the name of the form we're using, `CommentForm`. First up is `post()`: we use `get_object()` from
`SingleObjectMixin` that lets us grab the article `pk` from the URL. Next is `form_valid()`, which is
called when form validation has succeeded. Before we save our comment to the database we have
to specify the article it belongs. Initially we save the form but set `commit` to `False` because in the
next line we associate the correct article with the form object. Then in the following line we save
the form. Finally we return it as part of `form_valid()`. The final module is `get_success_url()`
which is called after the form data is saved. We just redirect the user to the current page in this
case.

And we're done! Go ahead and load your articles page now, make sure to refresh the page, then
try to submit a second comment.

Submit comment in form

It should automatically reload the page with the new comment displayed like this:

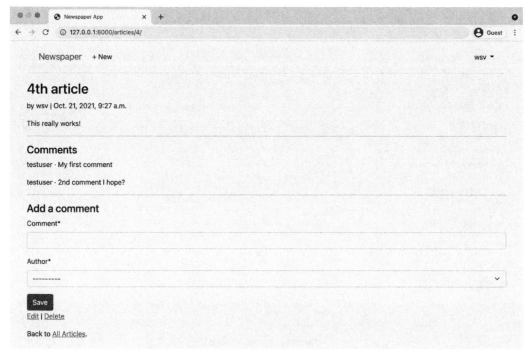

Comment Displayed

Conclusion

Our *Newspaper* app is now complete. It has a robust user authentication flow that uses a custom user model and email. Improved styling thanks to Bootstrap, articles, and comments. We even dipped our toes into permissions and authorizations.

Our remaining task is to deploy it online. Our deployment process has grown in complexity with each successive application, but we're still taking shortcuts around security and performance. In the next chapter, we'll see how to properly deploy a Django site by using environment variables, PostgreSQL, and additional settings.

Chapter 16: Deployment

There is a fundamental tension between the ease-of-use desired in a local Django development environment and the security and performance necessary in a production environment. Django is designed to make web developers's lives easier and it therefore defaults to a local configuration when the `startproject` command is first run. We've seen this in the use of SQLite as the file-based database and the various configurations in `settings.py` out of the box.

But as we've already seen in our projects, deployment requires additional steps for proper security and performance. Here is the complete deployment checklist last used for the *Blog* app back in Chapter 7:

- install `Gunicorn`
- create a `requirements.txt` file
- update `ALLOWED_HOSTS` in `django_project/settings.py`
- create a `Procfile` file
- create a `runtime.txt` file
- configure static files, install `whitenoise`, and run `collectstatic`
- create and update a `.gitignore` file
- create a new Heroku project, push the code to it, and start a dyno web process

In truth, though, this list is far from complete. We've relied on a number of shortcuts in our deployments so far that now need to be fixed. As the Django deployment checklist[170] notes, at the very minimum, a production environment should also have:

- `DEBUG` set to `False`
- `SECRET_KEY` actually kept secret
- a production database, not SQLite

---

[170] https://docs.djangoproject.com/en/4.0/howto/deployment/checklist/

The question is: how do we balance both of these needs? One environment for local development and another for production? Today, the best practice is to use *environment variables*, which can be loaded into the codebase at runtime yet not stored in the source code. In other words, even if someone had access to your GitHub repo and all the source code, they couldn't do much damage because the environment variables representing the most important details would be stored elsewhere!

In this final chapter we will switch over to environment variables and create a deployment checklist suitable for a professional website.

Environment Variables

There are multiple ways to work with environment variables in Python but for this project we'll use the environs[171] package. It allows us to create a dedicated `.env` file for environment variables as well as load a number of Django-specific additional packages to help with configuration.

On the command line, install `environs[django]`. Note that you'll probably need to add single quotes, `''`, around the package if you're using Zsh as your terminal shell, so run `python -m pip install 'environs[django]==9.3.5'`.

Shell

```
(.venv) > python -m pip install 'environs[django]==9.3.5'
```

Then, in `django_project/settings.py` there are three lines of imports to add near the top of the file.

---

[171]https://github.com/sloria/environs

Code

```
# django_project/settings.py
from pathlib import Path
from environs import Env  # new

env = Env()  # new
env.read_env()  # new
```

Next up, create a new file called `.env` in the root project directory which will contain our environment variables. We already know that any file or directory starting with a period, `.`, will be treated as a *hidden file* and not displayed by default during a directory listing. The file still exists though and needs to be added to a `.gitignore` file to avoid being added to our Git source control.

Go ahead and create a new `.gitignore` file with your text editor in the root project directory. Its contents should include our new `.env` file and also the `.venv` directory.

.gitignore

```
.venv
.env
```

While we're at it there are several other files and folders that are convenient to ignore for Python and Django development. These include all `*.pyc` files and the `__pycache__` directory. If you're on a Mac, there's no need to track `.DS_Store` which stores information about folder settings.

The final file to ignore is our local database contained in `db.sqlite3`. This file can become quite large and contains our *entire* database. We do not want someone with access to our source code to also have access to all our data. For convenience, we have used SQLite as our production database in previous chapters–that is, deployed on Heroku–but here we will switch over to production-ready PostgreSQL instead for deployment.

Here is what the final `.gitignore` file should contain:

.gitignore

```
.venv
.env
__pycache__/
db.sqlite3
.DS_Store  # Mac only
```

Remember that before we can apply Git commits we first must initialize a new directory with git init. Let's do that now. Check the status to confirm our .gitignore file is working properly and create an initial commit.

Shell

```
(.venv) > git init
(.venv) > git status
(.venv) > git add -A
(.venv) > git commit -m "initial commit"
```

It is a good idea to commit early and often on your projects.

DEBUG & ALLOWED HOSTS

It's time to configure our environment variable for DEBUG, which by default is set to True. This is helpful for local development, but a major security issue if deployed into production. For example, if you start up the local server with python manage.py runserver and navigate to a page that does not exist, like http://127.0.0.1:8000/debug, you'll see the following:

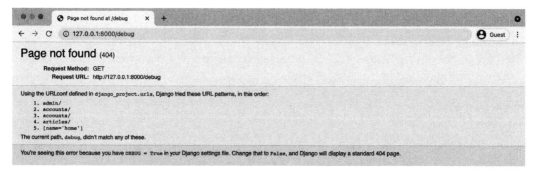

Page Not Found

This page lists all the URLs tried and apps loaded, which is a treasure map for any hacker attempting to break into your site. You'll even see that on the bottom of the error page, it says that Django will display a standard 404 page if DEBUG=False. Within the django_project/settings.py file, change DEBUG to be False.

Code

```
# django_project/settings.py
DEBUG = False
```

Oops! If you look at the command line, Django is complaining about a CommandError and has automatically stopped the local server.

Shell

```
CommandError: You must set settings.ALLOWED_HOSTS if DEBUG is False.
```

Because DEBUG is set to False, Django assumes we're trying to push the project into production and comes with a number of warnings like this. ALLOWED_HOSTS should be set to accept both local ports (localhost and 127.0.0.1) as well as .herokuapp.com for its Heroku deployment. We can add all three routes to our config.

Code

```
# django_project/settings.py
ALLOWED_HOSTS = [".herokuapp.com", "localhost", "127.0.0.1"]  # new
```

Re-run the python manage.py runserver command and refresh the page. The descriptive error message is no longer there! Instead, it has been replaced by a generic "Not Found" message.

Our goal is for DEBUG to be True for local development, but set to False in production. The two-step process for adding any environment variable is to first add it to the .env file and then to django_project/settings.py.

Within the .env file create a new environment variable called DEBUG. We will set its value to True.

.env
```
DEBUG=True
```

Then in django_project/settings.py, change the DEBUG setting to read the variable "DEBUG" from the .env file.

Code
```
# django_project/settings.py
DEBUG = env.bool("DEBUG")
```

It's easy to be confused here. Our environment variable is named DEBUG, the same as the setting it replaces. But we could have named our environment variable ANYTHING instead. That would have looked like this:

.env
```
ANYTHING=True
```

Code
```
# django_project/settings.py
DEBUG = env.bool("ANYTHING")
```

ANYTHING is a variable so it can have almost any name we desire. In practice, however, most developers will name the environment variable to match the name of the setting it replaces. We will do the same so DEBUG=True.

One more best practice we will adopt is to set a default value, in this case False, meaning that if an environment variable can't be found, our production setting will be used. It's a best practice to default to production settings since they are more secure and if something goes wrong in our code, we won't default to exposing all our secrets out in the open.

The final django_project/settings.py line therefore looks as follows:

Code

```
# django_project/settings.py
DEBUG = env.bool("DEBUG", default=False)
```

If you refresh the webpage at `http://127.0.0.1:8000/debug`, you'll see the full error page is back again. Everything is working properly.

SECRET_KEY

The next environment variable to set is our `SECRET_KEY`, a random 50 character string generated each time `startproject` is run. Starting in Django 3.0 the key begins with `django-insecure` as an additional prompt to tell developers not to use this specific key in production. Here is the `django_project/settings.py` value of the `SECRET_KEY` in my project. Yours will be different.

Code

```
# django_project/settings.py
SECRET_KEY = "django-insecure-3$k(g9eheqqbzr@#&tt)r6%ab-g1=!j@2c^y7*sl6+ltzys05!"
```

And here it is, without the double quotes, in the `.env` file.

.env

```
DEBUG=True
SECRET_KEY=django-insecure-3$k(g9eheqqbzr@#&tt)r6%ab-g1=!j@2c^y7*sl6+ltzys05!
```

Update `django_project/settings.py` so that `SECRET_KEY` points to this new environment variable.

Code

```
# django_project/settings.py
SECRET_KEY = env.str("SECRET_KEY")
```

Our `SECRET_KEY` is now out of the `settings.py` file and it is safe, right? Actually *no*! Because we made an earlier Git commit the value is stored in our Git history no matter what we do. Uh oh.

The solution is to create a new SECRET_KEY and adding it to the .env file. One way to generate a new one is by invoking Python's built-in secrets[172] module by running `python -c 'import secrets; print(secrets.token_urlsafe())'` on the command line.

Shell

```
(.venv) > python -c "import secrets; print(secrets.token_urlsafe())"
imDnfLXy-8Y-YozfJmP2Rw_81YA_qx1XKl5FeY0mXyY
```

Copy and paste this new value into the .env file.

.env

```
DEBUG=True
SECRET_KEY-imDnfLXy-8Y-YozfJmP?Rw_81YA_qx1XKl5FeY0mXyY
```

Now restart the local server with `python manage.py runserver` and refresh your website. It will work with the new SECRET_KEY loaded from the .env file but *not* tracked by Git since .env is in the .gitignore file.

DATABASES

Our current DATABASES configuration is for SQLite, but we want to be able to switch to PostgreSQL for production on Heroku. When we installed environs[django] earlier, the Django "goodies" included the elegant dj-database-url[173] package, which takes all the database configurations needed for our database, SQLite or PostgreSQL, and creates a DATABASE_URL environment variable.

The updated DATABASES configuration uses dj_db_url from environs[django] to help parse DATABASE_URL and looks as follows:

---

[172]https://docs.python.org/3/library/secrets.html
[173]https://github.com/jacobian/dj-database-url

Code

```
# django_project/settings.py
DATABASES = {
    "default": env.dj_db_url("DATABASE_URL")
}
```

That's it! All we need to do now is specify SQL as the local `DATABASE_URL` value in the .env file.

.env

```
DEBUG=True
SECRET_KEY=imDnfLXy-8Y-YozfJmP2Rw_81YA_qx1XKl5FeY0mXyY
DATABASE_URL=sqlite:///db.sqlite3
```

I hope you're wondering now: how do we set `DATABASE_URL` in production on Heroku? It turns out that when Heroku provisions a new PostgreSQL database, it automatically creates a configuration variable for it named ... `DATABASE_URL`. Since the .env file is not committed to production, our Django project on Heroku will instead use this PostgreSQL configuration. Pretty elegant, no?

The last step is to install Psycopg[174], a database adapter that lets Python apps talk to PostgreSQL databases. If you are on macOS it is necessary to install PostgreSQL first via Homebrew and then `psycopg2`.

Shell

```
# Windows
(.venv) > python -m pip install psycopg2==2.9.3

# macOS
(.venv) % brew install postgresql
(.venv) % python -m pip install psycopg2==2.9.3
```

We can use this approach because Django's ORM (Object Relational Mapper) translates our `models.py` code from Python into the database backend of choice. This works *almost* all the time without error. It is possible for weird bugs to creep up and it is recommended on a professional project to install PostgreSQL locally, too, to avoid them.

---

[174]https://www.psycopg.org/docs/

Static Files

Surprisingly, we actually don't have any static files in our *Newspaper* app at this point. We've relied entirely on hosted Bootstrap rather than our own CSS and JavaScript as we did in the *Blog* app. That is likely to change as the site grows in the future so we may as well set up static files properly now.

Stop the local server with `Control+c` and create a new `static` folder in the same directory as `manage.py`. Then add folders for `css` and `javascript`.

Shell

```
(.venv) > mkdir static
(.venv) > mkdir static/css
(.venv) > mkdir static/js
```

A quirk of Git is that by default it will not track directories that do not contain files. So when we push our code to both GitHub and Heroku these empty directories will not appear! This can cause problems since Heroku automatically runs `collectstatic` on the server, trying to combine static directories.

There are two solutions. One approach is to add a `.keep` file to an otherwise empty directory. Git will see this file and make the directory and file part of the next commit. However, since it is likely we will have files in here in the future, it is simpler to just create new files now to solve the issue. Let's do that. With your text editor, create new blank files called `static/css/base.css` and also `static/js/base.js`.

Next we'll also need to install the WhiteNoise[175] package since Django does not support serving static files in production itself.

Shell

```
(.venv) > python -m pip install whitenoise==5.3.0
```

WhiteNoise must be added to `django_project/settings.py` in the following locations:

---

[175]http://whitenoise.evans.io/en/stable/

- whitenoise above `django.contrib.staticfiles` in `INSTALLED_APPS`

- `WhiteNoiseMiddleware` above `CommonMiddleware`

- `STATICFILES_STORAGE` configuration pointing to WhiteNoise

Code

```
# django_project/settings.py
INSTALLED_APPS = [
    ...
    "whitenoise.runserver_nostatic",  # new
    "django.contrib.staticfiles",
]

MIDDLEWARE = [
    "django.middleware.security.SecurityMiddleware",
    "django.contrib.sessions.middleware.SessionMiddleware",
    "whitenoise.middleware.WhiteNoiseMiddleware",  # new
    ...
]

STATIC_URL = "/static/"
STATICFILES_DIRS = [BASE_DIR / "static"]  # new
STATIC_ROOT = BASE_DIR / "staticfiles"  # new
STATICFILES_STORAGE =
    "whitenoise.storage.CompressedManifestStaticFilesStorage"  # new
```

Run the `collectstatic` command for the first time to compile all the static file directories and files into one self-contained unit suitable for deployment.

Shell

```
(.venv) > python manage.py collectstatic
```

As a final step, in order for our templates to display any static files, they must be loaded in so add `{% load static %}` to the top of the `base.html` file.

Code

```
<!-- templates/base.html -->
{% load static %}
<!DOCTYPE html>
...
```

Deployment Checklist

It's easy to lose track of all the steps required for readying a Django website for production. That's why our checklist exists! We haven't installed Gunicorn yet as the production web server so do that now.

Shell

```
(.venv) > python -m pip install gunicorn==20.1.0
```

We also have not created a `requirements.txt` file with all the packages installed in our local virtual environment. We can do that as well.

Shell

```
(.venv) > python -m pip freeze > requirements.txt
```

Here is what the contents of my `requirements.txt` file look like. Yours might look slightly different: for example, Django will likely be on a 4.1.1 or later release because we installed it using ~= which means the latest 4.0.x version is installed. As I'm writing this book right after Django 4.0 has been released, the current version is still just 4.0.

requirements.txt

```
asgiref==3.4.1
crispy-bootstrap5==0.6
dj-database-url==0.5.0
dj-email-url==1.0.2
Django==4.0
django-cache-url==3.2.3
django-crispy-forms==1.13.0
environs==9.3.5
gunicorn==20.1.0
marshmallow==3.14.1
psycopg2==2.9.3
python-dotenv==0.19.2
sqlparse==0.4.2
whitenoise==5.3.0
```

We also need a `Procfile` file since we're using Heroku. This must be created in the base directory next to the `manage.py` file. Do so now in your text editor and add the following line to it:

Procfile

```
web: gunicorn django_project.wsgi --log-file -
```

And finally create a new `runtime.txt` file in the same base directory as the `Procfile` to specify what version of Python Heroku should use.use the following format. Make sure everything is lowercased!

runtime.txt

```
python-3.10.2
```

Here is a recap of what we've done so far:

- add environment variables via `environs[django]`
- set `DEBUG` to `False`
- set `ALLOWED_HOSTS`
- use environment variable for `SECRET_KEY`
- update `DATABASES` to use SQLite locally and PostgreSQL in production

- configure static files
- install `whitenoise` for static file hosting
- install `gunicorn` for a production web server
- create a `requirements.txt` file
- create a `Procfile` for Heroku
- create a `runtime.txt` to set the Python version on Heroku

Aside from the `Procfile` file and perhaps the `runtime.txt` file all these steps are necessary for a proper Django deployment on any platform provider.

GitHub

As a best practice, create a repository on GitHub to store the code as well. Create a new GitHub repo[176] called `news-app`. Make sure to select the "Private" radio button and then click on the "Create repository" button. On the next page, scroll down to where it says "â€¦or push an existing repository from the command line." Copy and paste the two commands there into your terminal.

It should look like the below albeit instead of `wsvincent` as the username it will be your GitHub username.

Shell

```
(.venv) > git remote add origin https://github.com/wsvincent/news-app.git
(.venv) > git push -u origin main
```

All set! Now we can configure Heroku and finally see our Newspaper project live.

Heroku Deployment

Make sure that you are already logged into your Heroku account via the command line.

---

[176]https://github.com/new

Shell

```
(.venv) > heroku login
```

The command `heroku create` makes a new container for our app to live in and by default, Heroku will assign a random name. You can specify a custom name, as we are doing here, but it must be *unique on Heroku*. Mine is called `dfb-news` so that name is already taken; you need another combination of letters and numbers!

Shell

```
(.venv) > heroku create dfb-news
```

So far so good. A new step at this point is creating a PostgreSQL database on Heroku itself, which we haven't done before. Heroku has its own hosted PostgreSQL databases we can use which come in multiple tiers. For a learning project like this, the free `hobby-dev` tier is more than adequate. Run the following command to create this new database. Replace `dfb-news` with your own custom name.

Shell

```
(.venv) > heroku addons:create heroku-postgresql:hobby-dev -a dfb-news
Creating heroku-postgresql:hobby-dev on â¬¢ dfb-news... free
Database has been created and is available
 ! This database is empty. If upgrading, you can transfer
 ! data from another database with pg:copy
Created postgresql-symmetrical-16853 as DATABASE_URL
Use heroku addons:docs heroku-postgresql to view documentation
```

Did you see that Heroku has created a custom `DATABASE_URL` to access the database? For mine here, it is `postgresql-symmetrical-16853`. This is automatically available as a configuration variable within Heroku once we deploy. That's why we don't need to set an environment variable for `DATABASE_URL` in production. We also don't need to set `DEBUG` to `False` because that is the default value in our `django_project/settings.py` file. The only environment variable to manually add to Heroku is `SECRET_KEY`, so copy its value from your `.env` file and run the `config:set` command, placing the value of the `SECRET_KEY` itself within double quotes "".

Shell

```
(.venv) > heroku config:set SECRET_KEY="imDnfLXy-8Y-YozfJmP2Rw_81YA_qx1XKl5FeY0mXyY"
```

Now it's time to push our code up to Heroku itself and start a web process so our Heroku dyno is running.

Shell

```
(.venv) > git push heroku main
(.venv) > heroku ps:scale web=1
```

The URL of your new app will be in the command line output or you can run `heroku open` to find it.

But if you go to this URL now though you'll see a 500 Server Error message! That's because the PostgreSQL database exists but has not been setup yet! Previously we used SQLite in production, which is file-based, and was already configured locally and then pushed up to Heroku. But this PostgreSQL database of ours is brand new! Heroku has all our code but we haven't configured this production database yet.

The same process used locally of running `migrate`, creating a `superuser` account, and entering blog posts in the admin must be followed again. To run a command with Heroku, as opposed to locally, prefix it with `heroku run`.

Shell

```
(.venv) > heroku run python manage.py migrate
(.venv) > heroku run python manage.py createsuperuser
```

You will need to log into the live admin site to add newspaper entries and comments since, again, this is a brand-new database and not related to our local SQLite one.

For larger sites, there are techniques such as using fixtures[177] or factories[178] to load data into a local database but doing so is beyond our scope here.

Refresh your live website and it should work correctly. Note that since the production server will run constantly in the background, you do *not* need to use the `runserver` command on Heroku.

---

[177]https://docs.djangoproject.com/en/4.0/howto/initial-data/
[178]https://docs.djangoproject.com/en/4.0/topics/testing/advanced/#django.test.RequestFactory

Conclusion

Phew! We just covered *a ton* of material so it's likely you feel overwhelmed right now. That's normal. There are many steps involved to configure a website for proper deployment. The good news is that this same list of production settings will hold true for almost every Django project. Don't worry about memorizing all the steps.

After you've built and deployed several Django websites, these steps will soon feel very familiar. And in fact, we've only scratched the surface of additional security measures that can be configured. Django comes with its own deployment checklist[179] that can be run via the command line to highlight additional security issues.

Shell

```
(.venv) > heroku run python manage.py check --deploy
```

The other big stumbling block for newcomers is becoming comfortable with the difference between local and production environments. It's very likely you will forget at some point to push code changes into production and spend minutes or hours wondering why the change isn't live on your site. Or even worse, you'll make changes to your local SQLite database and expect them to magically appear in the production PostgreSQL database. It's part of the learning process. But Django really does make it much smoother than it otherwise would be. And now you know enough to confidently deploy any Django project online.

---

[179]https://docs.djangoproject.com/en/4.0/howto/deployment/checklist/

Conclusion

Congratulations on finishing *Django for Beginners*! After starting from absolute zero we've now built five different web applications from scratch and covered all the major features of Django: templates, views, urls, users, models, security, testing, and deployment. You now have the knowledge to go off and build your own modern websites with Django.

As with any new skill, it's important to practice and apply what you've just learned. The CRUD (Create-Read-Update-Delete) functionality in our *Blog* and *Newspaper* sites is common in many, many other web applications. For example, can you make a Todo List web application? A Twitter or Facebook clone? You already have all the tools you need. When you're starting out I believe the best approach is to build as many small projects as possible and incrementally add complexity and research new things.

Next Steps

We explored a lot of Django material in this book but there is still much more to learn. This is especially true if you want to build large websites that must handle thousands or millions of visitors at a time. Django itself is more than capable of this. I've written a follow-up book called Django for Professionals[180] that tackles many of the challenges around building truly *production-ready* websites such as using Docker, a production database locally like PostgreSQL, advanced user registration, security, performance, and much more.

Django is also frequently used to create back-end APIs consumable by either mobile apps (iOS/Android) or websites that use a dedicated JavaScript front-end framework such as Vue, React, or Angular. Thanks to the power of Django REST Framework[181], a third-party app that is tightly coupled with Django itself, it is possible to transform any existing Django website into an

---

[180]https://djangoforprofessionals.com
[181]https://www.django-rest-framework.org

API with a minimal amount of code. If you'd like to learn more, I've written an entire book on the topic called Django for APIs[182].

3rd Party Packages

As we've seen in this book, 3rd party packages are a vital part of the Django ecosystem especially when it comes to deployment or improvements around user registration. It's not uncommon for a professional Django website to rely on literally dozens of such packages.

However, a word of caution is in order: don't blindly install and use 3rd party packages just because it saves a small amount of time now. Every additional package introduces another dependency, another risk that its maintainer won't fix every bug or won't keep up to date with the latest version of Django. Take the time to understand what it is doing.

If you'd like to view more packages, the Django Packages[183] website is a comprehensive resource of all available third party apps. For a more curated list of packages the awesome-django[184] repo is worth a look.

Learning Resources

As you become more comfortable with Django and web development in general, you'll find the official Django documentation[185] and source code[186] increasingly valuable. I refer to both on an almost daily basis. There is also the official Django forum[187], a great resource albeit underutilized resource for Django-specific questions.

You might also look at the DjangoX[188] and DRFX[189] starter projects to speed up the development of new projects.

---

[182]https://djangoforapis.com
[183]https://djangopackages.org/
[184]https://github.com/wsvincent/awesome-django
[185]https://www.djangoproject.com/
[186]https://github.com/django/django
[187]https://forum.djangoproject.com/
[188]https://github.com/wsvincent/djangox
[189]https://github.com/wsvincent/drfx

If you're interested in a podcast on Django, I co-host Django Chat[190], which features interviews with leading developers and topic deep-dives. And I co-write a weekly newsletter, Django News[191], filled with news, articles, tutorials, and more all about Django.

Python Books

Django is, ultimately, just Python so if your Python skills could use improvement there are two books in particular I recommend. For beginners and those new to Python, it doesn't get much better than Eric Matthes's Python Crash Course[192]. For intermediate to advanced developers, Fluent Python[193] and Effective Python[194] are worthy of additional study.

Feedback

If you purchased this book on Amazon, please consider leaving an honest review. For whatever reason, technical readers are often hesitant to write a review yet they make make an enormous impact on book sales and help me continue to teach Django.

As a final note, I'd love to hear your thoughts about the book. It is a constant work-in-progress and the detailed feedback I receive from readers helps me continue to improve it. I try to respond to every email and can be reached at will@wsvincent.com.

Thank you for reading the book and good luck on your journey with Django!

---

[190]https://djangochat.com

[191]https://django-news.com

[192]http://amzn.to/2okggMH

[193]http://amzn.to/2ovfgsR

[194]http://amzn.to/2nCqivT

Printed in Great Britain
by Amazon

85126923R00181